A Glimmer of Pixie Dust

Finding Our Hope in the Disney Story

Kate Grasso

Disney Cicerone

CONTENTS

Dedication   VII

Finding Our Pixie Dust   IX

Take Up Space   1

1. I Think I Can   3

The Smallest Castle   7

2. The View From Above   9

Taking Up Space   15

3. Let the Birds Be   17

4. She's Not a Bride   23

See and Be Seen   29

A Wave is a Simple Gesture   33

5. Why We Belong   37

6. When Mary Found Her Colors   43

Becoming Dapper   49

7. The Meaning Behind the Buffeteria   51

Haunted   57

8. Alice on the Shelf 59

Be Fearless 69

9. Somewhere Safe 71

The Carrousel Horse 75

10. Choosing a New Horse 79

The Flagpole's Tale 85

11. Who Cares 89

On Big Thunder 95

Dear Tony Baxter 97

12. Being Ruffled-up 101

13. Finding Freedom in the Frontier 107

Permission to Fly 115

14. The Open Drawbridge 119

It's a Small World After All 125

15. Animating Forces 127

Facing Villains 133

Unfurling the Sails 137

16. When Nothing is Going Right 139

The Fake Lampposts 145

Finding #42 149

A New Friend 153

17. Where We All Begin 157

Embrace Change   161

The Water is Still Now   163

18. The Disappearing Act   167

Ghosts of Disneyland Past   173

Being Stretched   175

In the Portrait Gallery   179

19. Go Another Way   183

On the Mark Twain   187

From this Island   191

A Pirate's Life for Me   195

20. The Splash Mountain Problem   197

On the Skyliner   203

21. Moving America   205

In Town Square   213

Keep Moving Forward   217

Pacing Mickey Mouse Park   219

22. The Dalmatian Disaster   221

Twilight Thoughts   229

23. No Time for Rest   231

Yale's Fireflies   237

24. Eliminating Contradictions   239

In the Push and Pull   245

25. Thinking Beyond the Basement   247

26. We Can't Go Back   253

Build This   259

27. (Don't) Stick to Shorts   263

Folly   269

Ghostly Resolutions   271

28. Predicting the Future   275

A Closed Window   281

29. Waiting by Walls   285

Starting Over   291

Author's Note   293

About the author   297

Also by Kate Grasso   299

Bibliography   303

To all those who are weary of waiting by walls.

Finding Our Pixie Dust

It's a cry I've heard over and over recently, the lament that our whole world feels like one unending, unprecedented event after another. Sometimes it feels like we are treading water just to get through the day, the week, the month, or the moment.

But then we step into the Disney parks or put on our favorite Disney movie, and suddenly we are transported. Not merely escaping, though some could call it that. No, the transformation we feel is tangible, as if the magic of the worlds these artists created is knitting our bones back together. It reminds us of our resiliency. Our capacity to endure, overcome, accept what is, and step confidently into a life where we know we are fully worthy of the space we occupy.

Disney is more than churros and changes that ruffle our feathers. It's less an escape from our broken world and more a healing of our broken selves.

The words you'll find here are ones inspired by Disney artists and Imagineers who were (and are) real people. They didn't live in a vacuum. They knew what it was like to feel joy, hope, fear, shame, struggle, and heartbreak. They knew, and they poured it into their work.

And that's the gift, the pixie dust they left behind for us to discover. Hope in the midst of change. Confidence despite critics. A way forward when we feel stuck.

Disney's history has, over time, changed the very fabric of American culture. But more importantly, it's changed *us*.

As you move through this collection of curated writings—some composed while waiting in long lines for attractions in the Disney parks—may you find the hope you need tucked into the corners of these forgotten stories. May they be the glimmer of pixie dust that helps you find joy, healing, and comfort. And may they remind you that, with the addition of a little faith and trust, there is always, always, *always* a way to keep moving forward.

Take Up Space

I

I Think I Can

The crows flew overhead and I took a deep breath in, inhaling the crisp evening air as my little Casey Jr. Circus Train wove its way around miniature storybook scenes and picturesque waterways. The water sparkled below me as strangers floating by waved from their pastel boats. I waved back from my perch in the caboose (my seat of choice) and marveled at how removed I was from every care and worry, hoping my little engine could pull me up over the hill.

(Spoiler alert: it could.)

That little train was around from some of the earliest concepts of Disneyland, intertwined with a canal ride. They called it Lilliputian Land, and though it went through quite a few changes in both location and theme, it exists in Disneyland today in an unassuming corner of Fantasyland behind Dumbo. So unassuming, in fact, that I often hear of people asking me where my footage is from and that they didn't know the ride was there.

But it's been there all along.

Casey Jr. Circus Train, like Beverly Park owner David Bradley once said to Walt Disney, is a ride that happens to you. Walt often hung out at Beverly Park in Los Angeles with his two daughters. He studied all its rides and features so intently that one day David approached him and asked what he was doing. David was happy to answer Walt's questions, and Walt then hired him as a consultant for Disneyland which was still in its early development. Walt had never designed a theme park before, and could use all the practical advice he could get. David, by the way, was also the one who suggested a hub plaza and convinced Walt to not have the midway-style games of chance typical in existing amusement parks because they only rip off guests (to which Walt agreed). So, thanks, David, for that.

(We do, by the way, have midway games in some of the Disney theme parks now, but those arrived long after Walt passed away. His strong anti-amusement park convictions have long since faded away from the company culture.)

When the Casey Jr. theme was being finalized, Walt suggested that the train should be able to talk and interact with the kids, wishing them "Happy Birthday" and whatnot while it was loading at the station. David called it a stupid idea because everyone would want to talk to the train and it would never be able to operate as intended. Walt relented, and they compromised by adding narration between Timothy Mouse and Casey Jr. into the soundtrack instead.

The Timothy Mouse part of the narration disappeared in the 1983 remodel of Fantasyland when the ringmaster's voice was added instead. Casey's voice is still present, however, in parts of the ride like the "I think I can" ascent over the hill. The voice you hear from Casey Jr. is the same one you hear in Disney's 1941 animated film *Dumbo*, and it's actually one of a female actress by the name of Margaret Wright. Her voice was distorted by using something called a Sonovox, a novelty sound effect made popular in the 1940s. As an early version of the talk box (something musicians use to modify sound), a Sonovox translated vibrations from the larynx into sound by holding up the device to a person's throat while they spoke.

Despite his objections to some of Walt's ideas, David was invaluable to Walt as a consultant. The idea of rides happening *to* you instead of you simply experiencing them is one that I've held onto over the years. Rides and spaces that feel immersive give us a sense of being disconnected from what holds us down. It allows us to move freely into a space where anything is possible. Attractions help us suspend reality, making the impossible possible. When I board the Casey Jr. Circus Train, I am not simply a human riding on a miniature railway. I am winding through the countryside next to friendly people in canal boats, allowing miniature versions of the stories I love to charm me and remind me that not everything in life is as overwhelming as I feel it is at times.

And when I get to the hill, to a challenge that feels too hard to summit, I know there is never a time when I can't make it over.

But only because I think I can.

Casey Jr. takes us on that journey, of struggle but remaining hopeful through the struggle.

Our everyday lives don't often resemble an evening ride on Casey Jr. Circus Train. Often it's more like the pile of crashed dishes in the *Sword and the Stone* (which actually borrows its sound effect from the little train that could). Perhaps that's why we savor the evening breeze ruffling our hair as we speed around a giant's quilt made of succulents and stained glass windows on tiny churches. We yearn for easier times, for transformative places. Places that happen to us in ways that make us stronger and more hopeful than all the other things that happen to us that are the exact opposite.

We need to be reminded that we *can*.

We *can* get out of bed in the morning.

We *can* do big, scary things that feel like too much.

We *can* choose forgiveness when anger and bitterness feel easier.

We *can* find our purpose in a world that too often tells us we don't matter.

We *can* climb that hill, whatever the current struggle might be, if only we believe that we *can*.

Because the best life is the one that happens to you.

But you have to first believe you are worthy of it.

The Smallest Castle

People have made her small over time

but she wasn't always that way.

Sleeping Beauty Castle started her life

as majestic and towering

confident and stately

a beacon of hope and safety

for all the people in every land.

Over time, trees grew

as did mountains and buildings

and consequently, she shrunk

as the words and labels of those

who compare sized her up without context or concern

But the circumstances around her

did not diminish her value

nor steal her beauty

and while some may call her names

or make assumptions about her character

she knows who she is

who she's always been

and she stands taller because of it.

2

THE VIEW FROM ABOVE

Climbing the stairs to the Adventureland Treehouse, my mind seemed to clear one step at a time as I slowly rose above the chaos below. The sun was sinking on the horizon, and guests started to look like tiny ants hurrying to and fro, a kinetic frenzy of activity that I was grateful to have a reprieve from for a moment.

Up at the top, I paused at the balcony outside the music room, resting my arms on the wood railing to look out over the view before me.

The one that's changed again and again, and yet is still the same.

Just like me.

Embedded in my brain are images of the past, and I inserted them one by one into the scene below. Ghosts of Mike Fink's Keel Boats and phantom fishermen on piers, a wishing well outside of the Chicken Plantation Restaurant to the left, and the shape of Casa de Fritos, the birthplace of our much-beloved Doritos tortilla chips, just out of sight to the right.

Subtle shifts, but shifts all the same.

Yet I wouldn't have thought about it at all unless I had made the climb up all of these stairs, changing my perspective.

Walt Disney did this too, sometimes. When they were building Disneyland, they erected large towers around the job site on which they mounted cameras to record all of the construction progress (something all of us Disney history nerds are so grateful for today). There is a record of Walt climbing up these towers and surveying the progress (or lack thereof) at times.

Once Disneyland was finally completed and guests started pouring into the parks, Walt watched from above through his firehouse apartment window, marveling at the sight and grateful that the stars of the show had finally arrived.

I think it's no accident that Disneyland's pre-opening prospectus stated that taking a grand circle tour on the Sante Fe & Disneyland Railroad *first* was the correct way to tour the park *before* taking that glorious walk down Main Street U.S.A. Riding the rails around the perimeter of Disneyland, you get a completely different view of the park than you do by foot. From your perch on top of the 8-15 foot berm, the dirt pulled from the Rivers of America forms a barrier to the outside world. It also raises your perspective, allowing you to see vistas and views you can't see any other way.

As I was riding on the railroad the other day, I realized that the height also allowed me to see something I'd never noticed before.

In Walt Disney World's Magic Kingdom, there is a prominent lookout tower on the top of the Fire Station, a feature I always thought was unique to that version of the apartment, possibly to set it apart from

Walt's hidden apartment in the firehouse in Disneyland. But aboard the *C.K. Holliday*, named for Atchison, Topeka, and Sante Fe Railway founder Cyrus Kurtz Holliday, I saw it.

A lookout tower.

It sat tucked all the way in the back, hardly distinguishable from the front of the building. The tower, now only clearly visible from backstage, was once noticeable from onstage as well, back when Disneyland was younger. Its presence had been unmistakable and in plain view of guests, especially from the elevated platform of Main Street Station.

So what happened?

Well, Disneyland grew up.

The trees that started so small, the ones Disney purchased from people's front yards and requested in newspaper classifieds, became towering sentinels dwarfing pony-sized Main Street (and the rest of the park as well). As a result, today the lookout tower on the back of Walt's apartment is something you have to peek through branches to see, where it used to be a prominently visible feature.

This happened all over the park, too. Early Disneyland concepts showed the castle as a central feature; a visual anchor for people, orienting them so if they got lost they would always be able to find their way back to the castle. And this *used* to be true of Disneyland, where you could see Sleeping Beauty Castle from virtually anywhere in the park. But over time as the trees matured and grew, the small 77-foot castle slowly disappeared from view, sinking into the landscaping, altering the scale and making the towering fortress look smaller in comparison.

It seems inevitable that the view will always change as we grow, sometimes even in ways that take us completely by surprise.

Back in 2006 when I was newly married to my dear husband Eliot, we lived on a shoestring as he made his way through a Masters degree program in Ireland and I didn't have a work visa. I spent my time reading classic literature, taking long walks in the Limerick countryside beside the River Shannon, and planning the cheapest of budget trips around Europe. One such excursion was to Paris just before Christmas, and of course, we had to take the train to Marne-la-Vallée and see Disneyland Paris, just for a day (since that's all we could afford at the time).

It was a cold day, snowing on and off mixed with a chilly rain. We started our day by getting stuck on Big Thunder Mountain Railroad on the first lift hill, and subsequently getting evacuated. After walking through the long tunnel under the river back to the mainland, we procured some festive Mickey and Goofy hats and explored the park at a leisurely pace, discovering a new Disney that I'd never experienced before.

On our rambles around the Christmassy park, we wandered up to the second story of Sleeping Beauty Castle, looking on in awe at the beautiful stained glass windows that Peter Chapman had made for Euro Disney (later known as Disneyland Paris). I hadn't known then that Peter had also restored the stained glass for Notre Dame and Westminster Abbey, I just know that we looked at the windows with the same reverence.

But the moment that stuck in my memory from that trip was when we stepped out onto the balcony, just outside of the prince kissing Sleeping Beauty awake, because I was in significantly less awe.

The view was disappointing.

I was so used to the U.S. parks' commitment to hiding infrastructure with well-placed landscaping and go-away green that I had culture shock from seeing a view of air conditioning units on the top of the obvious show buildings of Fantasyland.

It wasn't magical. It pulled me right out of the storytelling. Broken was the illusion of being in a quaint village, in a fantasy land.

I was disappointed.

We still enjoyed our Disneyland Paris day immensely, don't get me wrong. But it colored my view of the park for many years, long after we returned to the States and Paris was more than half a day's travel away.

Eighteen years and three kids later, we returned to the "most beautiful Disney park" and I braced myself, remembering my perspective from above.

I shouldn't have been worried. Because, almost two decades later, Disneyland Paris hadn't changed all that much, but *I* had.

When I climbed the interior stairs of the castle and stepped out onto the balcony, I was in awe. All of my study of Imagineering, animation, and the history of the park made me see the view before me with completely new eyes.

I saw Disney artist Gustaf Tenngren's concept art for *Pinocchio* come to life perched on top of Les Voyages de Pinocchio. I spied the Imagineering influences of Ken Anderson and Tony Baxter in the medieval village and façade of the Snow White ride Blanche Neige Et Les Sept Nains, so similar to the one that had been created for Disneyland's Fantasyland overhaul in 1983. To my right, I spied the replica of Merlin's Magic shop, almost identical to the one present on the opening day of Disneyland in 1955.

I teared up a little.

Sure, not everything looked perfect. Construction walls adorned the whole right side of Fantasyland, and there were still visible HVAC units on the top of show buildings. But I didn't see them, not really, because I chose to focus on the beauty before me rather than the imperfections.

My view rose above my previous perspective, given time.

I think it's easy for us to get stuck in the way we've always seen something, believing that is the only way to look at it because it's all we've known. But changing our perspective, altering our view, is a choice we get to make.

Sometimes this takes time, and growth. We have to actively look for ways to rise above, to climb our treehouses, even when it's not the convenient route, so that we can find our way to a new view. Sometimes we need others to convince us to step into a Skyway bucket so that we can see our lives the way they do. And sometimes we just need to let our hearts heal enough that we can see beyond the pain of our current circumstance to the joy and beauty just beyond it.

If what you're looking at right now doesn't look appealing, instead of letting it color your world, start looking for stairs to climb. A train to ride. A Skyway bucket to board.

You might just find your own firehouse tower you never knew existed but was there all along.

Taking Up Space

For as long as I can remember, I've taken up space

I've been in the way of others who were more important

occupied places where I shouldn't stand

felt out of place and uncomfortable in my own skin.

I've said "sorry" for existing

as if I was inconveniencing others by doing so

and felt the anxiety of always being in someone else's way.

But then I think of all the things

that are out of place

but perfectly accepted

in a place I love

a petrified tree in the middle of a theme park

a settled Lafitte anchor with a view of the water

a borrowed gothic spire atop a Bavarian castle

no one tells them to leave

or move

or that they don't belong

in fact, without them, there would be loss

an empty hole where something of value once stood.

We are not lost objects without a home

we create new homes

wherever our feet take us

and so we, too, can stand

confident that the space we take up

was always meant for us to occupy.

Like a tree

Like an anchor

Like a spire

rooted in the truth

that we belong.

3

LET THE BIRDS BE

Someone once commented to me that they thought the Enchanted Tiki Room was a waste of space.

I balked at the idea that anyone could so despise the sweet little singing birds and their tiki counterparts. I argued that Adventureland was (in 1963) one of the smallest lands in the park. It was a four-acre space with only one acre accessible to guests due to the massive blueprint of the Jungle Cruise, and the Tiki Room only occupied a relatively small area of that accessible acre.

This particular critic didn't care: they hated the singing birds.

I argued that the Tiki Room held the first true audio-animatronics, birds in cages modeled after a similar mechanical one that Walt and Lillian had picked up in their travels. It still hangs in Walt's office today, a testament to how curiosity can lead to great things if allowed to roam free and explore.

The Tiki Room birds started their creative journey in Disneyland's lost Chinatown off of Main Street, though in that version they were nightingales in cages singing in a dinner show planned for the Chinese restaurant. A project that, by the way, was how the brilliant comedian Wally Boag ended up writing and voicing part of the script for the Tiki Room. He had done so for the wall-mounted talking dragons in the planned Chinese restaurant, and Walt loved it so much that, when it came time to sort out the Tiki Room show, he remembered Wally's talking dragons and assigned him to the project.

But I digress.

These sweet little Tiki birds were the animatronics that had helped them solidify the techniques of using magnetic tape to create movement. It was technology that had only been recently declassified from the Polaris submarine, which made those birds historically significant as well as a marvel of technology and ingenuity.

But my attempts to defend my feathered friends fell on deaf ears.

The commenter didn't care about any of it. In their mind, the attraction was a waste of space.

I had to walk away from that particular internet troll and unpack exactly why it made me so upset. At first, I thought it was just their frustrating lack of knowledge of the history and artistry that created such a unique attraction. Or maybe it was their cavalier attitude toward something that meant so much to many of us, like telling someone that their favorite old necklace from their grandma is garbage and deserves to see the bottom of a trash can. I considered maybe it was simply their lack of thought of all the memories that space holds for us. Maybe they didn't have the nostalgia of "singing like the birdies sing" with people who meant the world to them, but who were no longer there to sing along.

But no, it wasn't any of those things.

(Well, maybe it was some of those things, but that wasn't the main thing that made me angry).

It was the whole concept of taking up space.

Because *I* felt like the Tiki Room.

As long as I can remember, I've made myself small. I am acutely aware of always feeling like I'm in someone's way, no matter where I'm standing or what I'm doing. Standing and waiting for my mobile order? Someone probably needs to stand where I'm standing. Putting my suitcase in the overhead compartment on an airplane? One hundred people behind me are inconvenienced by my need to store my stuff. Taking a photo of the castle from just the right angle? Some family with their kids deserves to have that spot for a picture with their families (this is all, mind you, even when no one is around waiting for said spot).

Everywhere I go, I feel like I'm taking up space that would be better occupied by someone else.

But then I started wondering why I was apologizing for my presence. I was not hurting anyone by deciding to get in line again and take a second ride on Big Thunder Mountain Railroad, even though it felt like I'd already had my turn and I should let someone else ride in my place (ridiculous and illogical, I know, but that's where my mind goes). The guilt tried to weigh me down, that I was somehow robbing others of their space simply by existing in mine.

This (admittedly unhealthy) thought pattern made me think about all the "misplaced" items at Disney that one could easily point at and say "that doesn't belong there." The fossilized tree in the middle of Frontierland that Walt Disney bought for Lillian "for their anniversary" (he didn't, that was just a joke between them, it was always meant for Disneyland). The "authentic" anchor of Jean Lafitte that sits embedded in the promenade of New Orleans Square (moved from a previous location closer to the Golden Horseshoe). And the gothic Viollet-le-Duc spire, similar to the one that used to grace Notre Dame cathedral in Paris, that sits on the right side of Sleeping Beauty Castle simply because Walt wanted it there. It doesn't match the Bavarian architecture of the rest of the castle. There is no reason for it to be there atop the castle's chapel, except for one reason: Walt loved it.

It takes up space that could be used for something else. Something more. Something better.

But if the spire suddenly disappeared off of the castle, we would all feel its loss.

If the petrified tree was put back in the Pike Forest Fossil Beds (now the Florissant Fossil Beds), it would no longer feel complete.

If the anchor was tossed into the Rivers of America and no one could sit beside it, enjoying their popcorn or a crispy cinnamon churro, we would wonder where it went.

Those objects are all allowed to take up space at Disneyland.

So is the Tiki Room.

And so are you.

But the truth is you aren't taking up space—the truth is that you complete it.

And who you are isn't an inconvenience to others, it's a gift.

Your presence, your body, your being; your ideas, they are a *gift* to those around you.

It's time to raise your head up and sing a little louder, move a little freer, and be okay with being seen because you are what makes the world a beautiful place to the people in your orbit.

And they would miss you if you were gone.

I am going to do my best to claim the space I stand in as one I deserve to occupy. And by doing so, I am acknowledging that my existence has value, even if I don't always believe it. Even if others don't always treat me that way.

I hope you will do the same, rooting your feet like an anchor when you feel you should shuffle away.

Claiming the history that made you who you are, like a tree that still stands despite years of pressing and hardship.

Shining like that 24 karat-gold out-of-place spire, confident that you're right where you need to be.

No, the Tiki Room isn't wasting space.

It's completing it.

And so are you in any place you occupy.

4

SHE'S NOT A BRIDE

Have you ever had someone assume something about you that wasn't even close to the truth?

That happened to me once at Disneyland. As I walked into Frontierland from the plaza hub with the morning rope drop crowd, I was filming some ducks on the water in the pond to my left. While holding my phone, I kept pace with the mass of people around me, no doubt headed to Rise of the Resistance (I myself was bound for Big Thunder Mountain, hoping to capture some photos of old repurposed Mine Train Through Nature's Wonderland critters for our Distory with Kate & Kirk Podcast). I was careful, as always, to not slow down or stop while gathering the video of the ducks, thinking to myself as I captured it how my eight-year-old daughter would love to see it, because every time I took her to Disneyland, she always asked to see the "Duck Show." But my filming was interrupted when a woman loudly said, "I'm just going to go around you." Given that I hadn't impeded her (there was no way for me to go faster), I was taken aback.

Stunned, I turned beet red and struggled to find my words as the young woman dragged her significant other around me. Somehow I managed, "Was that really necessary to say?" Because I knew it wasn't. Anyone who spends any amount of time in a theme park knows you just go around people who are in your way, no comments necessary. Because we all shift and accommodate each other, practicing our patience as needed. Or, at least, most of us do.

She didn't.

The young woman tossed over her shoulder, "Get used to it, it's going to be happening to you all day." And then she was gone, weaving her way around others all headed in the same direction, no doubt throwing more barbs at others in her efforts to get ahead.

Her response blew me away.

I held back tears.

Never had I felt so unseen at Disney, and that includes all the times I've been run over by strollers. She didn't know that I do my best to put others first when it comes to filming content. She didn't know that I try to be polite and respectful to those around me so that what I do doesn't affect their time with their family. That I try to see the humanity of the people in my orbit and be obliging to what they need, including waiting for kids to go first to see something they like. I stick to the back corners of rooms and turn down the brightness of my phone on dark attractions, and try to do everything I possibly can to show care and concern for those around me.

But this person wasn't interested in that.

When something like this happens, our first instinct is to correct them. To defend our character. To be seen for who we are, and not who they assume us to be. Because we can't stand the thought that they would go on into the world, putting us in a box in their mind where we will live forever due to their inattention.

The truth is, we make judgments about others, telling ourselves stories about them that may or may not be true, but to us with limited information, we make assumptions and then treat it as fact.

Take the Haunted Mansion, for instance. The tiny woman dressed in white at the end of the attraction is often mistaken for a bride, a miniature version of Constance Hatchaway (or perhaps the Beating Heart Bride, the earlier iteration of the figure in the attic prior to 2006 who made her way back to the Disneyland version in 2025). If you happen to be wearing a MagicBand+, it illuminates red and vibrates in a heartbeat pattern as you exit the attraction, reinforcing this theory. But "Little Leota," as she is sometimes called, is actually her own unique persona, derived from a character in a movie combined with literary lore.

Imagineers Yale Gracey and Rolly Crump spent almost an entire year simply going to the movies and tinkering with weird scenes and effects as they were developing the Haunted Mansion. One of the films they viewed in 1965 was called *The Loved One*. This bizarre film, "with something to offend everyone" as the movie poster boldly (and accurately) stated, included a female character named Aimee Thanatogenous played by Anjanette Comer. This young lady worked in Whispering Glades mortuary, a location inspired by Forest Lawn Memorial Park in Glendale (where, incidentally, Walt Disney is currently resting in peace). Aimee was an assistant to the mortician and funeral director in the movie, and, like the rest of the women in similar roles at whispering glades, she wore white and had a white mourning veil as part of her work uniform.

It's this character that we see at the end of the Haunted Mansion, not the bride in the attic. She is dressed in white and holds a bouquet of flowers in her hand, not for the happiest day of her life, but rather in mourning, to place on a grave (which, by the way, makes sense for her placement in the crypt). But how do we know, truly, that she isn't the bride that everyone assumes she is?

Well, the proof is in the pudd... er, the projector. The start of her original projection film reel for her face from 1969 says "Ghost Hostess." Other blueprints refer to her as a "small female figure with blowing clothes," and maintenance records call her "Small Girl" or "Ghostess." (There is, by the way, a record of her being called "Little Leota" once in 1970 on the plans for the Walt Disney World version of the mansion. It has quotation marks around it, implying it's a nickname rather than an official title. Disneyland Paris also has signage backstage that calls her "Petite Leota").

It is important to note here that the Ghost Hostess looked much less like a bride when the attraction opened in 1969. Along the way, her outfit was changed from more of a cloak, clutching decaying flowers, to what we have now, which does, admittedly, look more bride-like in appearance. And so everyone has assumed that's what she is.

But that isn't the truth about the Ghost Hostess.

Sometimes people make judgments about who we are based on what they see, but that's not the whole story about who you are.

When that person decided I was impeding her path and deserved a "talking to," she didn't see me at all. She saw what she wanted to see, to make assumptions and make herself feel better about her decision to tear me down on her way to be first.

She called me a bride, but I was a Ghost Hostess.

If I'm honest with you, I was pretty thrown off by this interaction. I took a few clips on my way to Big Thunder but my heart wasn't in it. I was second-guessing myself, replaying the situation, and trying to figure out if I had truly been in the wrong somehow and was blind to it. I eventually came to the conclusion that no, she really just emotionally bulldozed me in the middle of the Happiest Place on Earth.

I took a deep breath and walked under the Big Thunder Mountain sign, reassembling my bravery for the wildest ride ahead.

And that's when it happened.

A Cast Member friend of mine was at the entrance, calling out my name with a big smile, and giving me the biggest hug.

I was seen.

Seen for who I was, not what someone assumed I was.

It was healing, that hug.

I wasn't an obstacle in someone's path.

I was loved and cared for.

People aren't always going to see your worth. They are going to run you over, emotionally or otherwise on their path to somewhere else, probably never thinking of you again. They will call you a bride, but you know your Ghostess status. You know the truth about your character, regardless of the voices who name you otherwise. Don't let their poor judgment eternally follow you home.

See & Be Seen

What you see on the outside

are pretty outfits

and funny stories

smiles, laughter, and friendship

hours in the sun surrounded by facts and history

podcast studios and polished content

books that bring a little pixie dust

and words of encouragement

all wrapped up in Disney magic.

But what you don't see

are hours of research that sometimes go nowhere

days on end of not enough sleep

as I try to balance being a mom, wife, author, creator, and podcaster even more days spent on airplanes,

or airports when my flights are delayed

packing and unpacking suitcases that sometimes go missing

rinse and repeat.

You don't see

endless comments criticizing my work

my life

my appearance

the weight of which I try to drop as quickly as possible

but sometimes it lingers.

You don't see the anxiety that comes with every post,

trying to anticipate what people will accuse me of getting wrong

or what I have to include to justify my story

or myself.

You don't see the lingering thoughts

wondering if some dismiss my words

because my voice holds female inflection

or because I'm wearing pretty clothes

as if dressing my body somehow empties my mind.

But the sum of what you see

both sides together

equal a human

chasing a dream

wanting my words to matter

turning my past pain into prose

and hoping all these pieces of history

can be cherished and remembered

as they reflect a bigger story

than is evident on the surface.

We are all a balance

of the seen and the unseen

light and dark

hope and hurt

some of us just hide it better than others.

But the truly beautiful part

is letting others see both sides of who you are

so that they have permission

to do the same.

See, and be seen.

Both.

A Wave is a Simple Gesture

A wave

is a simple gesture

a hand distantly connecting to another

a human doing the same.

If you wave to someone you do not know

in this day and age,

in most places

it's odd.

But somehow

in a land of yesterday, tomorrow, and fantasy,

it's beautiful

because we are all together in a place we love

and there we put aside our worries

our politics

our insecurities

and choose to acknowledge and celebrate another's presence

as they float

or steam

or ride by

young and old alike

and all the ages in between.

A wave

is a simple gesture

but to be seen

heals us

suddenly we're no longer invisible

so we raise an arm in return

with a smile on our face

because someone cared that we were there.

It's a mutual moment between strangers

that gives us hope

and reminds us that we aren't as alone

as we think we are.

5

WHY WE BELONG

If you hang around with Disney people long enough, you'll eventually hear almost all of them call the Disney parks their home. Some of us have home resorts or a particular park that just feels like "ours."

But why do we feel that way, especially in a place that isn't anything like our actual homes? Where does the sense of belonging come in?

Well, it's built right into the design.

In *New West* magazine (the same one that later featured an article that inspired the movie *Top Gun*), there was an article in 1978 that featured John Hench, who at the time was executive vice president and chief operating officer of WED Enterprises (later known as Walt Disney Imagineering). This unique piece of journalism delves into the fascinating psychology of Disneyland and how it was designed to intentionally evoke certain emotions in its guests.

Now, one could make the argument that this is terribly manipulative. Often I've heard those who don't understand Disney say that it's just a fake plastic world, grotesque in its perfection.

But what they don't realize is that it's that same perfection that we need in our lives, because so much of our world is the exact opposite.

John Hench put it this way: Disneyland was made by filmmakers who know all about order and organization. When you tell a story, you do it linearly, with scene one followed by scene two and so on. You wouldn't jump around from scene five to two to seven, or any other combination, because then the story wouldn't make sense.

But that is what our world often feels like. Large cities are full of bustling chaos, beautiful sculptures juxtaposed with fast food signs and ads for something someone wants us to buy. When we experience all of these unrelated things at once, it can create chaos in our minds. And our past experience with chaos in a historical context is that it often leads to conflict.

As humans, we are conflict-avoidant, purely out of our need for survival. Thus, the juxtaposition of unrelated visual stimuli becomes a sort of chaos that is psychologically threatening, even if we don't vocalize it as such. In short, it lacks order.

Disneyland is the opposite. It is well-ordered, like a movie, because it was designed by people who understood the necessity of placing the scenes in order and having them all relate to each other in one way or another. As John Hench put it, "The order here at Disneyland works on people, the sense of harmony. They feel more content here in a way they can't explain. You find strangers talking to each other here without any fear."

And it's true. This tangible harmony is one of the unique aspects of Disneyland, that we can wave to strangers and not have it be creepy like it would be in almost any other context. I can smile at another mom whose

38

toddler is twirling in a princess dress, and both of us can share a knowing look, acknowledging the joy and magic that the park sprinkles on young and old alike. We can chat with strangers in a queue (when we want to... my introverted friends and I often opt out of that) or smile at people as we walk by and not have them give us a wider berth.

Disneyland gives us freedom that way, to be kind and joyful alongside others who need it as much as we do.

Now, admittedly, not everyone is joyful and kind in the Disney parks. Some carry their outside baggage in, forgetting to set it aside for the day, and so conflict does occasionally creep into our home. But for the most part, Disneyland was conceived as a place of harmony.

John Hench describes it by saying that nothing in Disneyland has an identity of its own; everything is related to something else. Disneyland is designed to minimize the chaotic fragmentation that we experience in our normal, everyday lives. One side of Main Street is aware of the other side. Each land transitions into another in a seamless "crossfade" so that you aren't even aware of the change until it's happened to you. Every scene in Disneyland is carefully planned to relate to everything around it, creating a rare and unique sense of harmony and balance.

All of this is what creates a sense of peace for us, a feeling that everything makes sense. We can breathe a little easier as we move down Main Street knowing that all of the colors, shapes, movement, and design talk to each other in the same language. And it makes us want to speak that language, too.

But here's the thing: We already do.

Disneyland wasn't designed to be full of empty streets and motionless rides. It was created as a place for regular people to come and take off the outside world for a little while to experience pieces of joy with those they love most. People are as much a part of the story being told as the rivers and tiki rooms and white carousel horses. We are part of what creates the harmony of the space, the balance necessary to truly make it feel like a home.

And so that's why, when we step through that entrance tunnel, we feel a deep-seated sense of belonging.

Because we do.

Disneyland was made for us. To allow us a place to overcome adversity and win the day. To give us space to breathe in a world lacking visual contradiction. To soothe our souls when the friction of the outside world's chaos has scraped it raw.

But it's not merely an escape, as some might assume. It's more than that. As John Hench put it, "Entertainment is usually thought of as an escape from problems, and escape from responsibility, but what we are selling is not escapism, but reassurance."

Disneyland is your land–*our land*. It's home because it's safe. Peaceful. Harmonious.

It's our place of belonging, where we can go and stand in the same spot we did when we were six years old and feel the exact same way we did all those years ago.

Deep down, as Walt Disney once said, "All people are children." We long for the safety that Sleeping Beauty Castle represents. We need a place to go where everything just makes sense because too much of what we know every day doesn't.

Disneyland is our land, designed to make us feel at peace in every possible way.

And that's why it's our home.

6

WHEN MARY FOUND HER COLORS

(Trigger Warning: DV)

Innocent, smiling children. Bright colors. Modern shapes that seem so orderly and put together.

Smiling on the outside, broken on the inside.

That was Mary Blair.

She lent her artistic style to countless Disney movies and, by way of the films, the parks' attractions as well, like Alice in Wonderland and Splash Mountain.

Walt wanted "more Mary" in his films, more of her stylistic influence, much to the chagrin of the contingent of male animators at Disney Studios who, no doubt, wished there was less Mary so that their own work could shine. Among them was Lee Blair, Mary's husband, who was bitterly jealous of her talent and success that eclipsed his own.

He didn't want to stand in her shadow, so he made her stand in his. An alcoholic with a fierce temper, Lee took out his frustration on Mary and their two children in the darkest ways, painting permanent shadows on their lives with his fists.

But Mary kept painting. Kept creating. Kept letting her color palette speak all the words she couldn't say.

I can only think that it was the way she survived, kept putting one foot in front of the other. She made hundreds of small 5x6 concept art paintings for the studio, from Alice falling down dark rabbit holes to the iconic scene of Cinderella standing in her tattered pink dress, her beauty torn apart by her jealous stepsisters.

Her work was stunning. Evocative. And tragic, when you know her story.

It's not a story of pity, but rather of turning our tragedy into something beautiful. Because that's what Mary did; she created an entire world to escape from reality, and in doing so she gave us a place to escape to, as well.

The same was true of her most iconic attraction, the one that shouted who she was to the world, unapologetically.

It's a small world.

This attraction was developed in just 10 months for the 1964 World's Fair, but it was almost not developed at all. Everytime Pepsi-Cola called asking for Disney's help, Disneyland's construction boss Admiral Joe Fowler kept telling them they weren't interested in making it, mainly because they were so overwhelmed with the three attractions they were already creating for the fair. When Walt got a call directly from board member (and widow of past Pepsi-Cola president Alfred Steele) Joan

Crawford, he immediately agreed to make the ride as a fundraiser for UNICEF, a tribute to the children of the world.

Mary Blair wasn't the only one assigned to the massive job of creating this attraction. Many Imagineers at WED contributed their talents, among them Marc Davis, Alice Davis, Rolly Crump, and Joyce Carlson (who, by the way, worked on all of the versions of Small World that exist in the parks and is honored in the Walt Disney World version by a little Joyce doll under the Eiffel Tower).

Sometimes Mary and Marc would butt heads, and Joyce or Alice would get stuck in the middle of their arguments about creative direction. One such instance was when Mary wanted to add jewels to the king and queen chess pieces in the United Kingdom scene. Marc didn't want them, and told Mary as such *loudly*, but after he walked away believing he had gotten his way, Mary leaned over to Joyce and said, "Put the jewels on."

"I listened to Mary and didn't hear anything else," said Joyce of the incident.

Marc Davis wasn't an enemy of Mary's though, far from it. In fact, he was one of her biggest supporters when it came to creating Cinderella, encouraging his fellow animators to use her designs and integrating her work as much as possible into his animation.

But for how beautiful Mary's work was, she wasn't perfect. She struggled to translate the 2D artwork for the outdoor façade of it's a small world to 3D, and so she asked Rolly Crump for help. He made a few "filler pieces" of structures to tuck in among her stylistic buildings, and voila, the iconic geometric building was created. Rolly's kinetic spinning wheels plated in 24-karat gold were the pièce de résistance. Shimmering in the sun, they would tie the design together with the (now defunct) Tower of the Four Winds sculpture (a feature, by the way, that Rolly was more than happy to trash after the fair since engineers had "ruined it" by making the proportions too large.)

My favorite work of Mary's, though, at least when it comes to Small World, is her color palette in the South America room. Because that was where Mary's colors come from, the ones that had prompted Walt Disney to say she "knew about colors he had never heard of before." Well, not the room itself, but rather South America, more specifically the 1941 goodwill trip that Walt Disney and his animators took to help sway sentiment to the Allies rather than the Axis powers just before World War II. The hope was if locals could see Americans as friendly, creative people, perhaps it would help combat the propaganda that said otherwise.

It was a wildly successful trip, at least for Walt and his group of artists. They experienced local culture, foods, and dances, and came back with more inspiration than they knew what to do with. It inspired a plethora of works, among them *Saludos Amigos* and *The Three Caballeros*.

But for Mary, it inspired even more.

Before this trip, Mary had been a lovely artist, but her work was often muted landscapes featuring browns, blacks, and tans. If you look at her art from this time, she had not yet settled into the style we now know her for.

But Mary found color on this excursion to South America. The bright colors that surrounded her on a daily basis seemed to seep into her pores and pour out through her paintbrush. It changed her fundamentally as an artist.

She saw the world as a vibrant place beyond the shadow of her situation.

That isn't to say that she didn't give us plenty of dark, moody art after this time. But even the most moving concept art she created after this trip is filled with colors that make it expressive in a way that's hard to explain.

Because it came from inside her. The longing for innocence in every sweet cherub face. The joy she desired for herself and her children spilled out in colors that shouted happiness from the rooftops. The geometric designs that ordered her chaotic world in a way she could not.

People sometimes tell me they can't stand Small World, for the song or the length or the dolls or a million other reasons. But I wish they could see what I see.

It's not only a prayer for peace like the Sherman brothers composed for its signature song. It's a prayer that the child in all of us is still allowed to have their innocence. Their joy. Their hope. Even when the world around us has done everything it can to strip it away.

Mary gave us colors so that we could paint our own world like she did. We can see ourselves in the peace of the message that we aren't all that different, that we can see each other, or, more importantly, see the inner children that we used to be, the ones that we had forgotten about. And we can remind each other that it's okay to still be that child, that they deserve love and to be seen.

Becoming Dapper

This outfit is more than clothing.

When I put on this skirt

or this dress

or these ears

I get to step into a new skin

one that is braver than I am

wilder

more alive

one that doesn't care what the world thinks

and knows every ounce of her worth.

I get to embody the free fall of the Hollywood Tower Hotel

or the recklessness of the wildest ride

I can wish the heads off of those who hurt me

or shape-shift at will into someone who holds their head a little higher.

I can see more than just myself when I look in the mirror

dressed in magic

adorned in the stories that have brought me peace when I didn't feel
peaceful.

Most days I am bound

by the limits of my broken heart

but when I get to become someone else for a day

I remember that it's my choice

not just what I wear

but who I am

the power I hold

and I am transformed

by the magic

and the reminder that I can be whatever I want to be

if I simply believe it enough.

7

THE MEANING BEHIND THE BUFFETERIA

At the end of Main Street U.S.A., forever looking on in awe of Sleeping Beauty Castle, sits the iconic Plaza Inn Restaurant. Named for the street no one recognizes as a cross street (Plaza Street), its Victorian stylings elevate the hub with its crystal doors and gingerbread trimmings.

And it holds more than its fair share of history, humor, and heart.

But let's back up and start at the very beginning when Disneyland was first being built. Walt knew they needed concessions in his park, but he didn't have any experience (or interest) in developing restaurants himself. At the same time, the park needed money–badly. He'd cashed out a life insurance plan, made exhausting television deals with ABC, and even sold his vacation home at Smoke Tree Ranch (so beloved that he wore the "STR" logo embroidered on his tie, which can be seen on the Partner's statue in Disneyland's hub).

Enter C.V. Wood. One of the only early contributors to the success of Disneyland who does *not* have a window on Main Street U.S.A. because of his feuding with Walt and his shady business practices, shaking down shop owners for kickbacks. But love him or hate him, he was vital to procuring funding to make Disneyland a success, including securing sponsors for "Walt's Folly."

Getting sponsors in those early days was no small feat. No one wanted to invest in something that was so unknown and uncertain, and most big sponsors didn't see the benefit of advertising at Disneyland. When C.V. Wood asked the Santa Fe Railroad for $50,000 in exchange for a logo on the trains and water tower, travel posters in Main Street Station, and an office where people could purchase railroad tickets, they balked at the price. Up until that point, they had essentially advertised for free at other kiddie parks, supplying only the cost of the paint to install their logo.

Every sponsor C.V. Wood–or Woody to those who knew him–worked to secure fell through. Money was running out, and the future of Disneyland hung in the balance. Luckily, Woody's friend Fred Schumacher had some connections left over from his time at the 1939 New York World's Fair. That was how they found themselves standing in the presidential suite of Swift's Packing Company in Chicago, giving a Hail Mary pitch to the company's president. Woody expounded upon the benefits of investing, emphasizing that people would associate their good feelings of being on vacation with their company's brand. The president listened, but eventually, he had enough. He asked Woody and Fred to leave his office, which they did, dejected.

But not totally so.

Because Woody had a trick up his sleeve. He had "accidentally" left his briefcase in the president's office, betting on the fact that the executive just needed time to ruminate on the possibility for a moment but would eventually be intrigued enough to give in. Though the president was skeptical of his sudden reappearance and his story about the briefcase, he laughed about the incident and seemed to soften to Woody's ideas. He agreed to an annual $110,000 lease to sponsor a restaurant in Disneyland, and that first big sponsorship kicked off numerous others (including Santa Fe, for $50,000 no less).

And so Swift's Red Wagon Inn Restaurant came to be, capitalizing on those good vacation feelings with the advertising tagline "Gay memories become glamorous realities at the air-conditioned Red Wagon Restaurant."

The decor of the Red Wagon Inn was decadent, indeed; its history assembled in bits and pieces from a much older building than the one with fresh paint in 1955. Many of the elegant fixtures were taken from a Los Angeles Mansion at No. 20 St. James Park, originally built by Baroness Rosa Von Zimmerman in 1870. A 1955 press release from Disneyland touted these features proudly:

"An old mansion in Los Angeles supplied part of the interior for the Delmonico-style restaurant at the Disneyland Plaza. The house was purchased and dismantled, with interior wood paneling and stained glass windows, crystal chandeliers, and staircases receiving the utmost care, for most of the mansion's features were incorporated into Disneyland's Main Street. A stained glass ceiling which had been used on the mansion's third-floor solarium, hand-carved wood paneling, and newel posts from the mansion were prominent in the restaurant."

The food was no less decadent, featuring "sizzling steaks and juicy chops" and a whole host of mid-century standards like premium lamb chops with mint jelly, ham steak with a pineapple slice, roast young tom turkey, and grilled pork chops with spiced crab apple. The "Menu for Young Americans" had a variety of Disney animation-themed options from Monstro's halibut steak to Pluto's frankfurter. Even the infants at the table were included in the smorgasbord of meats, with options of "Swift's Meats for Babies," strained or chopped beef or veal for just 25 cents per can.

The sponsorship was a success, including not only the Red Wagon Inn but also a Chicken Plantation restaurant and Swift Market House on Main Street U.S.A. Walt even had a special V.I.P. room in the back of the Red Wagon restaurant where he would host dignitaries and celebrities visiting the park (a precursor to Club 33, which Walt dubbed his "Hideout").

As Disneyland proved successful over the years, Walt was slowly able to buy out partners and regain control of the park. The Red Wagon Inn's lease ended, and Swift moved out, allowing Walt to do what he liked with the place. And what he liked? Well, it was darn expensive.

Walt's renovation to create the new Plaza Inn restaurant cost $1.7 million and didn't spare any expense. As Emile Kuri, the Imagineer who helped decorate much of Disneyland, put it, "Walt wanted the Plaza Inn to be absolutely the most luxurious thing for the average family." For the Plaza Inn, Emile scoured salvage yards and antique shops, adding an 1820 marble console table, an 1840s gilded Louis XV clock from Versaille (with matching barometer), and an 18th-century French fruitwood cabinet. Walt explained this extravagance to Emile: "The average factory worker or truck driver can't afford luxury for himself or his family, so I want you to make the interior really luxurious."

But it wasn't the posh furnishings or the custom-made Baccarat crystal chandelier (that could be lowered on a wire for cleaning) that made The Plaza Inn so remarkable.

No, that would be the prices.

Walt not only wanted the "average Joe" to experience a taste of luxury, he wanted to make sure they could afford it, too. "Even our prices are going to be cafeteria prices," said Walt of the new "buffeteria" style of dining. The buffet eatery had another perk in Walt's eyes; it eliminated tipping. According to Dick Irvine, Walt "always hated the tipping situation" and did his best to eliminate the practice in Disneyland. If people were getting their own food and bringing it to their table, no tip was necessary for table service.

The idea of Walt wanting to look out for the working man is a sweet idea, one that was backed up by similar actions of being slow to raise ticket prices and wanting to give the public a "fair deal" for parking. But what I find most interesting about Walt Disney is that he often longed for the kind of life he could never have for himself.

The legendary Imagineer Tony Baxter tells the tale of how Walt would get into the Carnation truck or fire engine on Main Street in the mornings and just drive around the park before it opened. That was the only time he would get to truly enjoy the park as a guest because, during operating hours in Disneyland, he was so recognizable that people would stop him every few feet for autographs. So, he drove a truck around in the early morning hours, drinking in the peace of the park he created for others to enjoy.

Tony also recalled a quote of Walt waxing nostalgic about his brother Herbert who worked for the US Postal Service as a mail carrier, and how great it would be to drive a truck around all day. To us, that might sound a little bit crazy. How could the larger-than-life Walt Disney desire to be just "like the rest of us"? But when you think about it, it makes sense.

Walt Disney loved the simple life. His favorite foods involved chili and grilled cheese. He had a favorite blue cardigan he wore often and was a creature of habit when it came to his favorite drink (Scotch Mist) and favorite suits (made of Pendleton wool, of course). He doted on his daughters and poured his profits back into making more films, more rides, and more magic for us all.

The Plaza Inn is nowhere near the simple life; quite the opposite, in fact. But the meaning behind it is simple enough: Walt got a small taste of the "working class life" every morning at Disneyland, the kind of lifestyle that he'd lost after becoming a celebrity. And while he couldn't ever truly live that life again, he wanted those of us who can't usually afford it to experience the lavish lifestyle that is often out of our reach. Walt gave us a luxurious, but affordable, buffeteria to allow everyone to feel like "somebody" no matter what amount showed on their paycheck.

With one extravagant restaurant, Walt communicated the simplest truth of all: We all have value.

Haunted

Stepping into the space

where we are stretched beyond our comfort zone

we wonder why we chose this path

because all eyes are on us

and few are friendly.

We soldier forth down endless corridors

ignoring the cobwebs and the signs of failure

because this is where we need to be

in a space that reminds us of our mortality

of our fragility.

Summons to scary places make us want to run

and yet

when we join those who abandoned the shackles

of who they were supposed to be

their joy becomes ours

because it's not what we do that gives us our value

no title

no talent

no tale from our past

no matter how we cling to it

but rather who we are

that is what follows us home

a hitchhiker we choose

everyday.

And somewhere along the way

what we were afraid of

becomes something worth celebrating

because it pushed us into places

that made us realize

what haunts us makes us human

and our humanity rests in our peace.

8

ALICE ON THE SHELF

Poor Alice.

Every time I see her, I sigh at how little she was loved by the very hands that created her.

Well, not technically the *original* hands that created her, because that would be English novelist Lewis Carroll in 1856, with artist John Tenniel providing the 42 wood-engraved black-and-white illustrations for the novel *Alice's Adventures in Wonderland*.

But Walt Disney was fascinated by the story. He once said, "No story in English literature has intrigued me more than Lewis Carroll's *Alice in Wonderland*. It fascinated me the first time I read it as a schoolboy and as soon as I possibly could, after I started making animated cartoons, I acquired the film rights to it."

Before the *Alice in Wonderland* feature-length animation we all know and love, Walt was already well acquainted with Alice, starting with the *Alice Comedies* in 1923. The first one, a combined live-action and animation short called Alice's Wonderland, was a reverse take on Max

Fleisher's *Out of the Inkwell* series, which featured an animated character in a live-action world. In the *Alice Comedies*, Walt took a live-action character (in this case, a little girl named Virginia Davis) and put her in an animated world. The first short was so successful that it launched a series of 57 *Alice Comedies*, none of which turned out to be based on any of Lewis Carroll's writings.

In 1933, Walt Disney looked into making *Alice in Wonderland* into a feature film starring Mary Pickford, but quickly dropped the idea after Paramount Pictures released their own live-action version. After making a Mickey Mouse cartoon short in 1936 called *Through the Mirror* based on Lewis Carroll's *Through the Looking Glass*, Walt put Alice on the shelf for a while, instead choosing to focus his attention on creating *Snow White and the Seven Dwarfs*.

The world faced all kinds of change in the years that followed, as World War II altered everyone's sense of safety, perspective, and priority. Disney Studios was commandeered (so to speak) for the war effort, and Walt's artists were put to work making war propaganda films for the United States military. But after the war ended and life reset, Walt started thinking about Alice again. First, he brought in Ginger Rogers for a Records Personality Series recording. He brought in English author Aldous Huxley, author of *Brave New World*, and commissioned him to write a treatment for Alice for $7,500 (Huxley's mother, by the way, had once upon a time been photographed by Lewis Carroll as a child).

Huxley's live-action script starred Charles Dobson (the real name of Lewis Carroll) and described Alice as "temporarily an orphan at the mercy of a governess and an old man who do not truly understand or love her." In the 31 pages he presented to Disney in November of 1945, the script had Alice's caretakers locking her in a garden house where she'd imagine that objects were characters: a piece of rope became the caterpillar and a stuffed tiger became the Cheshire Cat. Alice even says her "system of overcoming fear is pretending to be in Wonderland."

Walt Disney decided not to use the script, proclaiming it "too literary" for his vision of the project. Story artist Joe Grant wasn't quite as diplomatic, stating it "only compounded the confusion." And so, once more, Alice was put on the shelf.

But not for long.

Walt decided that the whimsical Alice story would work best in an animated medium, but he was nervous about how the critics would perceive new drawings of these classic characters. He said in a letter to a New Jersey fan, "Practically everyone who has read and loved the book of necessity sees the Tenniel Alice, and no matter how closely we approximate her with a living Alice, I feel the result would be a disappointment."

Luckily, he had Mary Blair.

Mary's bold color styling and unique midcentury modern aesthetic lent itself well to the madcap romp through Wonderland. She worked alongside fellow artists Claude Coats, John Hench, Ken Anderson, and Don DaGradi to create the colors for the animated feature which would be, stylistically, a dramatic change for the Disney house style. John Hench brought to the film a sense of surrealism that he had developed from working closely with Salvador Dalí on the film *Destino* (canceled in 1946, but revived in 2003). Marc Davis animated the character of Alice. Disney's "Nine Old Men" broke the movie into scenes, bringing their own personalities into each one. With a culture full of ambition and rivalries, each animator tried to "out-crazy" the other, and the film soon turned into what animator Ward Kimball called "a vaudeville show."

Walt was optimistic at first. Before the film was released, he said, "Everything is looking swell here at the plant. Alice is just about ready to be wrapped up and I think it is about as good as can be done with it. I think it is going to be an exciting show. While it does have the tempo of a three-ring circus, it still has plenty of entertainment and it should satisfy everyone except a certain handful who can never be satisfied."

At the studio, however, Alice was looking decidedly more grim. Animation was a tedious process. Walt asked why it was taking everyone so much time to complete, and it was simply because it wasn't fun for the animators. Marc Davis struggled with the character, saying, "There [was] no opportunity for her to be warm; perhaps if she had [had] her cat with her. The entire cast is made up of these entirely unsympathetic characters who don't understand her, and she certainly doesn't understand them. It was very difficult to do."

Everyone felt relief when it was done. "None of us liked it when it first came out, and we thought it was a pretty poorly done film—and from a purist point of view, it is," Marc said of *Alice in Wonderland*. "It was a situation where you take this little girl and throw her into a madhouse ... at the time an awful lot of us had the feeling that we were disappointed in it. We always expected more of ourselves. We always expected everything to come off better than it did." Marc further explained, "I think part of that attitude came from Walt himself, which was, 'Oh, well, the next one will be better.'"

They weren't the only ones who were unsatisfied with it. When the movie was released in 1951, both the Lewis Carroll purists and those hoping for a new telling of the tale were bitterly disappointed and not shy of saying so. Critics lambasted the film, and it bombed at the box office. The studio lost $1 million on the film, erasing all the financial success and progress they had made from *Cinderella* in 1950.

After the failure of Alice, Walt vowed to never again take on a tamper-proof classic, and he was so discouraged by the film's lack of success that he said, "Someday I would like to reach the position where this company doesn't have to live from one picture to the next."

Thankfully, *Alice in Wonderland* did much better on subsequent cinematic runs, and today, as Marc would say, "There is an entire cult out there who thinks it's the greatest thing in the world."

But Alice didn't just struggle in the film. Her presence in the Disney parks has also had its share of ups and downs. An early concept for Fantasyland from 1954 shows a walk-through version of Alice that would have been next to Snow White and Her Adventures. During the pre-opening promotion for Disneyland, the attraction was described as a "Walk-through the wonderful experiences of Alice in Wonderland, as the White Rabbit takes you down the rabbit hole, through the maze of doors, the Rabbit's house, past The Singing Flowers, Dodo Rock, the Mad Hatter's Tea Party, [ending] in the courtroom of the Queen of Hearts."

But, once again, Alice was shelved.

Budget cuts and time constraints on building Disneyland in a single year made them eliminate this attraction for opening day, and instead delayed the project until 1958, when Alice became a ride-through experience instead. Claude Coats wanted to put people in cars made of playing cards, but Walt said, "No, make it a caterpillar," and so he did.

The 1958 version wasn't quite what we have today. It featured an oversized room and an upside-down room and had no Queen of Hearts at all. It ended with the Mad Tea Party (some of whose teacups were repurposed for the current version) and then after a brief interlude with an exploding cake, you'd crash through a series of progressively smaller and smaller doors until finally you burst through to the outside to the tune of a Goofy yell (which Claude Coats added simply to make people smile at the end of the attraction... it's still present today). Then you'd travel down the vine to the unload area, and that was it. As Bob Gurr put it, "The attraction was not very understandable."

The renovations to the ride in 1983 created a slightly more faithful (and less confusing) retelling of the story, adding the white rabbit, Tweedle Dee and Tweedle Dum, the playing cards, the Queen of Hearts, and Alice herself (who was a last-minute addition brought in from Walt Disney World, a backup character for the Mickey Mouse Review show).

The Mad Tea Party scene was added onto a new 600-foot section at the end of the ride, put there by Tony Baxter to remedy a childhood disappointment. In his own words, "Alice in Wonderland always intrigued me because half of it was outside. As a kid, I used to sit up there on Snow Mountain, which back then was just a mound of dirt called Holiday Hill with some benches. You could look down on Alice, and I was always fascinated with the track. It was convoluted and it seemed to lend itself as part of a Wonderland world, kind of crazy and eccentric. I thought that it was an amazing layout, but as a kid, I was always a little disappointed. You could see from the top of the vine that you just reach[ed] the ground and that was the end of the ride." To make sure no kids would ever be let down by the end of the ride again, he added a large exploding birthday cake to the end so that the ride "went out with a bang."

Over time the ride, like the film, became more and more beloved with age. Through the years it has been enhanced and refreshed with special effects and projections, and Alice herself even got an upgrade to an audio-animatronic instead of a forgotten storeroom spare.

It would seem that Alice was no longer put on the shelf.

And yet, in Walt Disney World, she was.

I often hear people lament the fact that the beautiful Alice in Wonderland ride is nowhere to be found in Disney World's Magic Kingdom. It did get the Mad Tea Party that was present in 1971 when the park opened (though they added a roof in 1973 when the rain became more of an issue than they had planned), but, alas, no Alice.

But they were supposed to have one, though, and an amazing one at that.

Imagineer Rolly Crump had been working on a slightly different version for Walt Disney World pre-opening, a ride that allowed you to travel through Wonderland and control your perspective. As he put it, "I thought it would be great if the ride vehicles were the tea cups. Just like the ones that are in Disneyland, I wanted you to be able to spin them on the ride, too. That way you'd be going through Wonderland, and you'd be able to spin around to see it from all angles. I always thought the movie was kind of crazy and wild, so I wanted to translate that into the ride. It would still have the same hourly capacity, which is what they were looking for, but it would've taken it to the next level, where I thought it needed to be."

As fun as that version would have been, Alice was sadly put on the shelf, yet again. Said Rolly, "It seemed to make a lot of sense to me, but not to management. Obviously, they didn't do that, or build an Alice dark ride at all at Walt Disney World." (They did, however, use this concept later for Roger Rabbit's Cartoon Spin, testing out the concept by putting a Mad Tea Party teacup on the track for Pinocchio to see how guests could control their perspective. But again, that was all in Disneyland, and not Walt Disney World).

Poor Alice.

When I see her and her adoring fans now, I wonder how many of them know about the struggle for her presence in Disney's world. She wasn't an instant hit like Mickey, nor an enchanting princess like Cinderella. She was a sad little girl with an active imagination and maybe not as much personality as we are used to from our Disney characters. But she carved out her niche and found her people. She just had to give it time.

Not everything we do is going to turn out perfectly. We aren't always going to be loved by everyone, and oftentimes it may feel like people do not understand us at all.

People certainly didn't understand Disney's Alice. They wanted her to be something else. Something they were familiar with. Something that made sense to them.

But the zany, madcap world of Alice in Wonderland resonates with those who feel out of place, who oftentimes find themselves "in a world of their own." It's an invitation to not be so put together, to be silly and wild and free, unapologetically who you are even if it goes against the grain of what you're supposed to do, say, or be.

As it turns out, Alice isn't so poor, after all. She's rich. Rich in color, rich in chaos, rich in imagination. She gives us permission to be ourselves, even if we look like a pair of eyeglasses with feet (thanks, Marc Davis).

Alice is all of us, lying down in the flowers for a while and sharing our thoughts. She's us, stomping our feet at what we don't understand. She's us, just wanting to find our way home.

We may not always be everyone's cup of tea, but that's the beautiful part about Wonderland. In a world full of unusual people, we get to boldly be our own brand of curiouser and curiouser, no excuses or apologies required.

(Almost) every day on this earth is your very merry unbirthday; don't forget to go out with a bang.

Be
Fearless

9

SOMEWHERE SAFE

There was no purpose for it, really.

An empty shell of a building in the center of Walt's theme park, not even an attraction you could pay admission to enter in 1955. That would come later.

And yet today, the castle is the most iconic symbol of the Disney parks we know. We simply must take a photo with it every trip to document our passing years and remember each happy day. It's what we crane our necks to see as we make the turn around Town Square—to catch a glimpse of its majesty sitting regally at the end of Main Street. And it's what we gaze at in awe of its simple beauty, perhaps wondering why it holds our attention the way it does.

John Hench had his own theories about our fascination with Disneyland's castle. In a 1978 article with New West magazine entitled "Disneyland Is Good For You," he discussed the castle's significance to us on an instinctual level. Castles have always been a place of safety, a stronghold that protected its community from ruffians and thugs and any other evil that could destroy the village people (that is, the people who live in the village, not the group of eclectically dressed singers).

Walt wanted the castle to be a visual anchor, something easily seen from all lands so that you could orient yourself and know how to get back to the plaza hub. Even with the shorter-than-planned 77-foot Sleeping Beauty Castle, this was true for a long while, as the vegetation took years to grow before it obstructed the sightlines as it does today.

The castle has also taken on a new, unexpected sense of meaning as well over the years: it's nostalgic. No matter what changes in the parks, the castle remains, steadfast and sturdy. I have stood before it again and again between ages two and twenty-two and beyond, gazing up at its spires and turrets. Each time, this simple structure has reminded me that it's okay to dream. To hope. To remember fondly how life used to be while looking ahead to how it will be, eventually.

When everything in life has felt like it's fallen apart, the castle still remains. It's unchanged. Whole.

Like we so often wish we were.

I love John Hench's way of summing up the visual psychology of the park. Order instead of chaos. Peace instead of heartache. A place where everything makes sense in a world where often nothing seems to do so. And at the center, the heart of this place we love, is a place of safety, a reminder that we aren't alone in our quest for survival. The castle is strength when we aren't strong. Trust when we can't trust. There for us when nothing else is.

When we face unexpected changes and our lives feel out of control, somehow this simple structure brings us back to ourselves. The two-year-old one and the twenty-two. Telling us we will be okay, and holding all the hope we can't bear to hold because it feels too heavy.

John Hench said that the main message of Disneyland is that there is "nothing to fear," and for a generation who had seen a few World Wars and a Great Depression, that message was sorely needed. But it is no less important to us as we crave consistency and assurance in a world full of pandemics, politics, and prices that creep up day after day.

When our everyday lives get tangled up in the mess of not knowing which way is up anymore, the castle gives us direction, the visual anchor that Walt wanted, but in a different way perhaps than intended. It not only gives us safety but reminds us of our own strength as well, our ability to do hard things and face challenges knowing that there is beauty on the other side. It's an embodiment of ourselves, our past and present and everything we could be, and a not-so-subtle nudge from Walt that "all our dreams can come true if we have the courage to pursue them."

I wish I could fold the castle up and put it in my pocket to carry with me on the days I feel less than strong. But knowing that it's there, waiting for me at the end of Main Street, offering a comfort and a peace all its own, that is enough. It's waiting for me, for *us*, every day, even if we are far from its gentle shadows and gleaming accents. It's there for us, always.

As a reminder of all our past selves that looked up at its spires with hope and wonder.

As a reminder that some things stay, even while others fade away.

As a reminder that we are, and always will be, okay.

The Carrousel Horse

I chose the horse with armor today

it felt fitting

because I wear my own

though no one can see it.

Outside I sparkle

confident and beautiful

as the gleaming gold accents on the carrousel

but inside I cower

afraid to be trampled again by those who stampede over my heart.

Some are obvious villains

dark horses who make no apologies for their darkness

they are less threatening than the ones disguised as allies

adorned with pretty features that hide their ferocity and deception.

My armor isn't part of me

it wasn't always there.

Others have required its placement

following tears and heartache.

I stoically affix each piece

and every so often check to make sure they are still in place

when someone new ventures too close

just in case

to survive unscathed.

But armor is a funny thing

because while it can protect my horse

and my heart

it also hides who I am

the true me

the one who has been made soft by the trauma of past battles

tender and compassionate underneath the sharp metal and shrapnel
embedded deep.

The part of me the world needs

is hidden under my armor

gently nudging me to dismount

and find a new horse

one who is prepared for love more than war.

Today I chose the horse with armor

but tomorrow

I hope to be strong enough

to choose the one without.

10

CHOOSING A NEW HORSE

Armor is a funny thing.

I wrote those words in my head from a place of heartache as I stepped aboard my carrousel horse in the Magic Kingdom, instinctively choosing one covered in gold armor, so much so that you could barely see the horse beneath. I'd had a conversation with an old friend that day that revealed just how much armor they themselves had acquired over the years. Maybe even more armor than they even realized, judging from the words that they said to me, spilling over with pain and regret.

As my horse slowly started its familiar spin round and round, I began to think about my own armor, the plates I've gathered over the years and attached to my person to protect myself from pain. Some from mistakes I've made, but more often from people who saw my unshielded self and opted for violence, whether purposefully or accidentally.

I started to wonder as the castle moved into sight and away again if safety is our ultimate goal. The castle certainly is such a place, as previously discussed. But we can't stay behind our protective walls forever; we must venture out into the world and make our way forward, even when doing so is a frightening prospect.

As my horse moved up and down, I thought of Walt Disney, and how he faced all kinds of betrayal in his life from people he trusted. Charles Mintz stole Oswald the Lucky Rabbit and many of Walt's animators right out from under him, men he'd trained and trusted to stick by his side.

It added a piece of armor, no doubt.

When Walt finally had a measure of success, he built a beautiful animation studio, with custom-made desks for the artists and windows that faced just the right direction to capture the light. He rewarded those who had been with him the longest, but doing so came at a price: the animators who felt they were not compensated as well as others decided to strike. Of course, as with any strike, it's more nuanced than that, but nevertheless, it led to yet another betrayal; people who Walt trusted walked out on him. People he'd thought of as friends.

Those who worked at the studio often tell the tale of how the strike changed something in Walt. The entire atmosphere shifted at Disney Studios, from being like family to being all about business. Gone was the convivial camaraderie that had been forged of late nights and creative consultations. In its place were protocols and professionalism.

More armor, hidden beneath suits and ties.

You can only take so much heartbreak before your heart gives up and goes numb.

Sometimes I wonder if this happened to Walt, to some degree. If you watch him over the course of his career, his early life is full of optimism, his demeanor jovial and enthusiastic. Over the years, however, he becomes more thoughtful and contemplative, turning inward. One could argue that age and experience have this effect on us all, which is true to an extent. But I think we also need to consider Walt's rise to fame in the equation.

When Walt received his Oscar for *Snow White* in 1939 (with seven tiny dwarf Oscar statuettes next to the main one), 10-year-old Shirley Temple noted that he seemed nervous. Though Mickey and the *Silly Symphonies* had done well for many years previous to the release of *Snow White* in 1937, Walt was still very much a simple country boy at heart (and diet) for most of his life up until that point. Suddenly, he was a celebrity, and with that comes all kinds of new armor one must adorn in order to survive such a lifestyle.

Your life is no longer your own when you become a public figure. People demand your time, your attention, your autograph, and, in many ways, your life. Your family becomes their business, your personal affairs, public knowledge. It's a mental health nightmare, and one no doubt every celebrity has to navigate carefully (and many don't, as evidenced by the sheer amount of tragic downfalls in Hollywood). You also have to learn who you can trust and who you can't.

Walt had his inner circle. His trusted family, friends, and colleagues who he knew he could share his life with safely. His nurse Hazel George who treated his old polo injury after work each day was one such person, calling his time with her his "laughing place."

It was a safe place to set down his armor, if only for a little while.

The reality is, none of us can walk through life without (way too many) bumps, bruises, and scars. People you thought were friends suddenly walk out of your life, sometimes with little to no explanation as to why. Or you choose to love people and they don't know how to love you back well, so your heart comes out the other side cowering and covered with a shiny new protective shell. Broken promises, heartbreak, and relational wounds are unfortunately par for the course as we make our way around the seasons, one by one, like the turning of the carrousel.

But while Walt no doubt was wounded by betrayals and disappointments, he didn't let his armor become so heavy that he couldn't see past it to hope for better. To keep telling stories with happy endings. To create places where families and people from all walks of life could set their armor down for a little while and be in a happy place where dreams come true.

Disneyland was and is a place of both acknowledging our fears, wounds, and past while also embracing the optimism that more is possible. It reminds us that the armor that we wear isn't permanent, that there are safe places, safe people, where less of it is necessary.

And when we climb onto a carrousel horse and it carries us in the familiar rhythm of around and around and up and down, we can revisit that time of our lives when no armor was necessary, if even for a moment. Back when our hearts were open to love without the worry of loss, and our arms could spread wide to embrace those around us without wondering if they would welcome it.

I don't know about you, but I want to love like my armor isn't necessary. I want to believe in happy endings, even when they feel impossible, and wave hello to people like they are all potential friends. I don't want to walk around bent under the weight of old wounds and those who didn't value me enough to stay.

I want more than a heavily armored life.

If that's you too, you get to make that choice. Are you going to keep choosing impenetrability and safety, or will you choose to reach out and be vulnerable, allowing someone to see what's hiding under your armor?

Because here's the thing: what you've been keeping safe might not be yours to keep.

Your goodness, your love, your kindness, your heart, they aren't meant to hide in the darkness. They were given to you so that you could share them with others. Perhaps people who don't know how to heal from their own wounds need someone who has been there to show them the way.

Someone brave.

Like you.

If you don't believe it and need a few more rides on the armored horse before you can choose another one, I get it. I do. Unburdening yourself is a process, one that can't be rushed.

But you, my dear Disney friend, you've done more than your fair share of heavily armored journeys around the carrousel.

I hope that someday you will see just how worthy you are of choosing a horse like Jingles. One adorned with bells in their mane instead of weighed down by heavy armor. And as you take in the world from your new perch, I hope you also discover what has always been true of you: that you are more than deserving of being happy and free.

The Flagpole's Tale

I was broken

run over by the careless

when I got in their way

and nobody seemed to notice.

I once radiated light

but then my world went dark

forever changed by someone who didn't see me

who didn't value my presence enough

not to tear me down

on their way to somewhere else

and so the circle of sunny yellow

I spun around me

instantly faded to black

my world forever changed.

But then

someone saw me

broken and bent

shattered and shadowed

and thought I was valuable

even when I didn't resemble who I had been.

They saw me at my worst

and only thought the best.

They brought me to a new place

one of boundless optimism

and settled me where I had a view of it all

joy and excitement

coming and going.

I held new colors

important ones.

People started to gather around me

hand held to their heart

and I felt a new honor and dignity

as I straightened my spine.

Words of a new beginning

were placed at my feet

and that's when I knew

that if I had not been broken

I would not be here

surrounded by happiness

living a new life

with more light

than I ever could have produced on my own.

II

WHO CARES

"Who cares?"

I've read those words so many times in my comment sections on social media that I eventually just added them as filtered words so my eyes wouldn't roll right out of my head.

It usually is a response to something I've posted that is horribly obscure in Disney history. Like the safety lamps you can see inside the mine tunnels of Big Thunder, lights covered in a metal mesh sleeve to absorb heat from the lamp's flame and prevent any errant gas in the depths of the mine from being ignited (a detail, by the way, I find delightfully ironic considering these lamps are present in the final lift hill when the dynamite does, in fact, ignite and explode). Or the often-overlooked hornbill in the lost and found of the Jungle Cruise that was lost and found himself. He was once in the attraction trying to escape being eaten by some crocodiles, then moved to the boathouse after the Indiana Jones attraction was added, and has now been "found" by the skippers, currently for sale perched above Trader Sam's.

I can understand why people say, "Who cares." I get it. I do.

In the big scheme of things, I suppose these details don't matter much. They don't fix any big problems in our world, or answer any of life's big questions. They are just fun pieces of creativity that we get to delight in when we discover them along the way. And yet, there are so many of us who spend our time in the Disney parks searching, learning, and seeking the small details as much as we glory in soaking up the castle views and majestic mountains.

I have many times stepped back to consider why I feel the way I do about Disney. Why am I obsessed about half-red half-white light bulbs on Main Street that Walt wanted in order for the repeating pattern to make sense? Why am I charmed by a broken lamp post that got a second chance at life by becoming a flagpole, honoring our veterans every evening? Why do I find myself gazing into a wishing well and getting teary at the thought that the voice singing back to me is the same one who amplified Walt's dream all those years ago? When Adriana Caselotti's sweet words echo in my ears, I can't help but pause and remember how she pleaded heavenward for Walt to help her find Snow White's voice, as time had made her vocal chords struggle to repeat her performance of her youth. After her entreaty to the man who said, "It's fun to do the impossible," she nailed the recording on her next take, and so we can now stand around the small wishing well and hear her voice. We have permission in that place to wish that we, too, would find the voice we need to fulfill our purpose, right when we need it the most.

Perhaps not everyone sees the park as I do, details and all. And, funnily enough, Imagineering knows that, and accommodates for all the levels of attention of its guests. When creating Disneyland, WED Enterprises had a unique method for designing the park: the four levels of detail.

Take the Haunted Mansion, for example. When you approach the building, you take in the overall vista: an antebellum mansion, based on the Shipley-Lydecker mansion in Baltimore, Maryland (that the early Imagineers got from an art book called *The Decorative Art of Victoria's Era* by Francis Lichten from 1950). It's a beautiful scene laced with a hint of the ominous, foreboding that we can't quite explain but is there nonetheless. That's the first level. When you approach the mansion, you start to take in the lawn, the pet cemetery, the wreath above the door (which briefly had a big spider web at one point in its history), and the cemeteries, that's the second level. You start to see more features, a clearer picture of just *why* it feels ominous.

As you step closer to the front porch, you notice the abandoned spyglass and empty chairs and tables on the second story (some of which used to be set with empty pitchers and drinking glasses), which make you curious about who lives here, and why they would abandon their leisure time. It forces you to confront the fact that there *should* be people here, because the evidence exists to prove their presence, and yet there are none to be seen.

The third level is also the point at which you would have–once upon a time–been able to catch the "traveling lights" moving from window to window on the second story (but only if you were patient and attentive). This odd phenomenon adds to your sense of unease, a feeling that something is here, even when you can't see evidence of anything living.

And so you creep, perhaps timidly, toward the entrance, and that is what brings us to the fourth level of detail. You notice that the decorative iron grating has birds on it, an off-the-rack "Birds of Paradise" design not unique to the Haunted Mansion. The door fixtures also have something found elsewhere, the word "Yale" emblazoned on the locks, a remnant from when Disney partnered with Yale & Towne. Their presence lingers from a time when Yale once outfitted the entire park with door knobs and locks (as well as having a shop on Main Street where you could get a pretty sweet souvenir key to Sleeping Beauty Castle).

One could easily see how the early Imagineers adopted this "four levels" technique directly from the filmmaking process. Long shots establish scenes from far away, medium shots give you a little more intimate perspective, and close-ups are for intensely focused attention.

The current Imagineers also design on different levels, but these are based less on the filmmaking perspective and more on the ways guests tour the park. Imagineer Kevin Lively once explained to me and my *Distory with Kate & Kirk* podcast co-host that when they design for current attractions, they have three levels they think about: waders, swimmers, and divers.

Waders are those who, perhaps, go to Disney more casually. They are in it for a few fun rides, some churros, and a photo in front of the castle. What they know about the Jungle Cruise, for example, is that it's a boat ride with corny jokes that is set in a vintage era. They might not even know it's called the Jungle Cruise, calling it more by its description like "the jungle boat ride." They are merely wading in the water of the immersive experience, aware that their surroundings are relaxing and fun and that is enough for them.

The swimmers are those who look a little closer. They know generally what the attraction is about, and know its name. They have spent some time observing the items in the queue and can repeat some of the jokes by heart. They know when to chant "O2H" for the backside of water and know better than to step over the center crates when loading and unloading.

And then we have the divers. That would be me, and possibly you, too, if you're reading something like this. We are the people who obsess about every item added to the queue. We care where the props came from, and that the blueprints hanging on the wall of the boathouse are from a never-realized bamboo shade version of the boats that were based on the 1953 movie *Mogambo*. We know the backstory and search for ways the Imagineers have woven it not only in the attraction, but Adventure-land and beyond. We love every detail, from the medicine bottles that reference other attractions to the same blue argyle socks that are placed in the second story in Disneyland and in the Lost and Found area in Walt Disney World.

The details matter to us. A great deal.

But why?

Because they tell us that our details matter, too. That who we are, the unique, quirky, sometimes bizarre parts of ourselves are all worthy of being known. And the people who care about them, those who choose to see us for who we truly are, they are worth holding onto because they *get* us, oddities and all.

The details we find and share and obsess over at Disney permit us to embrace all the parts of ourselves that we keep hidden away, that we don't always show to those around us because we wonder if they will care. If they will accept who we *really* are, even if that includes an obsession over a hornbill or a gorilla reaching for bananas instead of punching an alligator, or photos in the queue that reference Stanley Kubrick's 1980 horror film *The Shining* (that's in the Walt Disney World version, by the way, and it features a delightful photoshopped face of Kevin Lively instead of Jack Nicholson front and center).

The details make us happy because discovering them is like finding hidden treasure.

But guess what: that's how people feel about your details, too. The people who matter, anyway, will care about what you love. Who you are. What you obsess over. Maybe they won't exactly share your passion for light bulbs or wishing wells, but they will love that *you* do because it's part of you.

Those who care about your details are the ones who matter.

Don't be afraid to filter out the ones who don't.

On Big Thunder

I.M. Fearless

I.M. Brave

words I don't feel as I step into this new journey.

I'm scared, if I'm honest

of what is on the other side of this darkness

twists and turns I can't anticipate

coyotes and cacti waiting on the sidelines

and I am flying

holding on through this wildest ride in the wilderness.

But somewhere between the goats and gasps

I loosen my grip

and the danger simply becomes my next big adventure

my hands fly into the air as I let go

of every worry

of all the what-ifs

of all my uncertainty

and I am changed

splashing down into anticipation of what comes after this wild ride

embracing this new frontier

a land where everything was new to everyone

so it can be new to me, too.

I take one last look at the whistling trains

whipping around the mountain

and see more fearless riders with arms raised

bold, daring, and courageous

words that this place allows us to claim

mining our way into who we will become

one wild ride at a time.

Dear Tony Baxter

Dear Tony,

It must have been frustrating to be so young

wanting to be heard but wondering if you had a right to do more than
listen

trying to find your place at 22 in the shadow of Walt's legacy

cobbling together a new idea from pieces of older ones

fragments from the original dream-builders

of the park that you loved.

It must have been heartbreaking to watch your detailed models go into
storage

becoming another antiquated Western story gathering dust

as the space race took center stage

and the future became trendier than the past.

It must have been exciting the day you dusted off that same miniature
mountain

even if it had to change its location, father west

as you searched National Geographics for charming hoodoos

making adjustments to fit a new space

as you must have to step into a new role.

It must have been terrifying to know you had the power to mess up
Walt's park

to remove beavers and bears and blacklights

to dismantle childhood memories

and beloved rainbow caverns

yet have faith that it would all be worth it.

It must have been surreal

to step into a train birthed from your imagination

zipping past nods to the legends before you

and watching your own dream become a reality

amidst howling coyotes and water splashes.

It was brave

building a mountain that Walt had never dreamed of

taking a risk that could have failed, but didn't

trusting that inner child

creating moments of hope that we, too, can be daring

as millions overcome fear and danger on a runaway train

for generations to come.

Dear Tony,

You were brave

so that we can be courageous, bold, and fearless,

both on and off the ride that simultaneously grew us up

and let us be kids again.

Thank you for giving us Big Thunder Mountain.

12

BEING RUFFLED-UP

It was just an ordinary morning at Disneyland in the 1960s. Everyone was working in the early morning light to get the park ready for the day, making sure everything was picture-perfect for guests. Custodial staff washed streets and swept stores. Fresh-squeezed Valencia orange juice was being prepared in the Sunkist Citrus House, one basketful at a time. Paint was retouched where it had been chipped from the burden of contact with thousands of people. And all around the park, ride vehicles were being tested and retested, getting ready for a full day of toting guests through imaginary worlds and landscapes.

Over at the Mine Train Through Nature's Wonderland attraction, maintenance crews had another task to do to make their ride show-ready: preparing the animals.

The 200 animatronic animals added to this slow-moving train ride attraction in 1960 (when it changed from Rainbow Caverns Mine Train to the Nature's Wonderland version) were a challenge, and that's putting it lightly. Some of them didn't last long in the attraction because of their difficulties.

101

For example, Bob Gurr created what he called his "best and most believable animal ever," the animated mountain sheep. It was designed to walk out from behind a rock and greet guests on the Pack Mule Train, an attraction where guests could ride real burros on tour through the Rainbow Desert shared by the Mine Train attraction. But when WED (Imagineering) put the sheep into action for the first time, it turned out that this sheep was a little *too* realistic, because the lead mule startled and reared back, toppling off of the ledge and into the Rivers of America, taking all of the mules (and guests) along for the ride. They tried again a week later, to see if it was just a fluke, but the mules had been so spooked that they stopped dead in their tracks at the spot where the sheep would appear and refused to move forward (apparently they didn't like being jump-scared by a sheep). So the sheep was removed, despite it being a terrific, believable animal in Nature's Wonderland.

It wasn't the only animal that was a little too believable. Up in the trees, they perched a few animatronic ravens that featured simple movement, their electronic mechanisms often hidden inside the branches they sat upon. The local bird population, however, was not thrilled with these new intruders in their roosting territory, and they took to attacking them any chance they got.

And then there was the bounding deer, which never really worked at all. Bob Gurr had designed an animatronic deer to look like Bambi bounding through the forest, traversing a triangular course on a wheeled carriage to achieve the effect. But unfortunately the design included a wired rope to pull the deer through the course, and it had a habit of unwinding every few days, halting the deer's progress. Bob called it his "worst design disaster of all time," and said that anyone who actually saw it in action was lucky, indeed.

But for all the animals that didn't work, there were hundreds that did. Rainbow trout jumped through the water in Bear Country, with one having been so unfortunate as to be caught in the mouth of a bear in the water (you can still see one of them jumping today, by the way, in the pond across from the side of Big Thunder Mountain Railroad). Other bears lined the banks of the water, either climbing the trees or scratching their backs on the rough bark (thanks to Marc Davis, who conceptualized many of these animal gags). Beaver worked hard on gnawing logs for their dams, and one swam in diligent circles in the water, forever busy as a... well, you know.

One animal, though, is not often talked about in Disney history. It was a simple set of critters designed by Marc Davis that he had planned to stage on the side of Cascade Peak. But their final home ended up in a different location, popping up and saying hello to guests above a tunnel the train passed through on its way to Big Thunder Falls.

And of course, we could only be talking about Disney's long-lost colony of marmots.

They were simple, really. Each marmot would pop up from a hole in the ground one at a time while whistling at the guests (which marmots tend to do when alarmed to warn their colony of impending danger). A narration could be heard aboard the train, claiming they were whistling at all the "pretty gals" on the train before it rolled underneath the critters' home towards Cascade Peak.

But on this particular morning in Disneyland, the marmots weren't set in motion quite yet. Cast member Jimmy Walker was doing his part to make the show ready for guests, using a general issue brush to tidy the marmot's fur. Over and over he brushed each one in turn, clearing the hairs on the marmots of dust and debris, and making sure the fibers were neat and straight.

So involved was he with his attention to the marmots that he didn't realize a man was walking up behind him. And that man, wandering the tracks for an early morning inspection of the ride, was none other than Walt Disney.

Walt took one look at the marmots, shook his head, and said, "You don't do it that way, they're supposed to be all ruffled up when they come up."

Shocked by Walt's presence and possibly embarrassed by his mistake, Jimmy went back to each marmot and did what Walt asked, re-ruffling the marmots.

Walt knew that an unruffled marmot wasn't a believable one. If they wanted people to believe the marmots were real, their fur would never, in nature, be groomed to perfection. They would look a little worn and disheveled like they had been foraging for food or tussling with one another. While many animals do have fussy grooming regimens, it's rather unbelievable that an entire colony would look like they had just stepped out of an issue of Marmot GQ at the same time.

Perfect wasn't believable, and it certainly wasn't the goal. Walt knew that. While he wanted Disneyland to be picture-perfect in many ways, in some he knew that messier was actually better than flawlessly groomed.

And yet, this is what *we* are trained to do. Brush and polish and perfect ourselves until we look just how we think we should for the world to see us. We pretend we don't have rough edges, or bad days, or messy houses. We project a perfect life, a happy marriage, cherubic children, or glamorous careers. We erase blemishes and filter out imperfections until we blur out any semblance of real life.

But because that version of us isn't really who we are in our everyday lives, it often feels disingenuous. Hollow.

We wonder, would people still love us if they saw the truth of who we were? And are we brave enough to show them?

I believe they not only would adore the realistic version of you, they would welcome it. They may even love you more, knowing that you were choosing to live your authentic ruffled-up marmot life with them instead of feeling the need to hide who you really are.

This is, of course, terrifying. There's a vulnerability in sharing our unfiltered selves. We risk rejection, ridicule, and judgment from the other seemingly unruffled people around us. But here's the thing: most of the negative things you think people will think about the *real* you are actually just all in your head. They are stories you are making up, lies that you tell yourself that keep your filter in place and your life stiflingly picture-perfect.

Being unruffled is easier than choosing a life of authenticity, but stepping out of our comfort zone into the sunlight of our imperfections gives us a freedom we didn't know we lacked until we feel the warmth of its rays on our skin.

Give people a chance to love the ruffled-up version of you. That version is beautiful because it's honest; imperfectly perfect. And being ruffled around others gives them permission to be their ruffled-up selves, too.

And before you know it, we slowly become a colony of ruffled-up marmots, whistling at the danger of chasing perfection because we know it's a threat, one we don't have time for anymore.

We're too busy basking in the sun of our imperfections, blissfully ruffled for all the world to see.

13

FINDING FREEDOM IN THE FRONTIER

It would be easy to call it one big mistake. A series of blunders. Poorly planned. Badly conceived.

Because the first version of Frontierland was a Wild West–but not in a good way.

Let's caulk our covered wagon and float it back to 1955 when Disneyland first opened. The Frontierland then looks quite a bit different than the one we are used to today. Sure, the sturdy wood fort still flanks the entrance. The trading post to the right is still there, though it was called the Frontier Trading Post until 1987 when it became Westward Ho Trading Co. (a reference to the 1956 Disney film *Westward Ho the Wagons!*). Before us, water is still flowing through the Rivers of America.

But that's where the similarities (mostly) end.

After stepping into the fort, on the left side where the Pioneer Mercantile exists today, was one of the earliest attractions to close in Disneyland: The Davy Crockett Frontier Museum. Inside, guests would find an exhibit about the legendary Battle of the Alamo which included life-size wax figures of Davy Crockett film actors Fess Parker and Buddy Ebsen. There was also a historical firearm display provided by the National Rifle Association.

This walk-through exhibit didn't last long. After only three short months, the unpopular museum was converted into a combination of retail space and interactive games, with its name changing to Davy Crockett Frontier Arcade when it reopened in 1956. As much as Walt Disney wanted Disneyland to be a place of learning as well as fun, the museum simply wasn't exciting enough to hold people's interest.

But that was just the start of the closures in Frontierland. Because while the trading post remained mostly unchanged throughout the decades, the spot next to it had a massive identity crisis.

Framed by a porch with 60 pine burlwood posts from Wyoming (that are now just fiberglass replicas of the originals), the Miniature Horse Corral was situated in the location that is now the Frontierland Shootin' Exposition. This was basically just a petting zoo, complete with Sardinian donkeys, ponies, and miniature horses from the Shetland Islands, one of which was named Lilly Belle after Walt's wife Lillian. While the animals were adorable, only a few guests were permitted in the corral at a time, which made it an extremely low-capacity attraction that took up a significant amount of real estate. That, combined with the fact that the animals were often hiding in the shade from the heat and the crowds, led to its closure in 1957.

Disney missed the mark, again.

And then there were the wagons and the stagecoaches.

Guests could climb aboard a Conestoga wagon with the words "Oregon or Bust" or "Westward, Ho!" emblazoned on its canvas and experience life like a pioneer on the Oregon Trail (never mind that most of the pioneers walked since wagons were usually meant to carry provisions and not people). *The Pasadena Independent* reported in December 1955, "You will ride the Conestoga Wagon in Frontierland—one of the most picturesque and vital vehicles in history. It was the Conestoga, not the Covered Wagon, that developed the West. The great wagons were first built in the Conestoga Valley of Pennsylvania, with water-tight bottoms that permitted safe crossing of rivers."

But the iconic Conestoga Wagons were not the only way to tour the Old West by wheel in Disneyland. Children held on tight as they splashed through puddles bouncing on the back of rustic buckboard wagons. And while the sized-down replica stagecoaches were lovely, not everyone got to ride inside them. During the loading process, a ladder was produced so guests could climb on top of the roof and perch precariously atop it for their ride through the Painted Desert.

It was madness by today's safety standards.

There were no safety restraints, no seatbelts, and they were all pulled by unpredictable animals that were sometimes frightened by the sound of the train, the *Mark Twain's* steamboat whistle, or even just ducks taking flight. Three separate accidents involving spooked horses were the nail in the coffin for the stagecoaches in Frontierland, including one where an empty coach pulled by panicked horses slammed into another that was loading guests, overturning the stagecoach and pinning the driver beneath it. Another coach carrying 17 people flipped over at Rainbow Bridge when the sound of the train's steam scared the horses. And a third incident injured ten people when frightened ponies pulled the undercarriage away from the stagecoach, causing it to collapse.

The decision to remove the stagecoaches and phase out the wagon rides couldn't have been an easy one for Walt Disney. One of his earliest concepts of Disneyland, called Mickey Mouse Park, featured a stagecoach prominently in the artwork. Walt himself loved to take the stagecoach around the park in its off-hours, offering rides to Imagineers and cast members. Claude Coats even recalled a time when he tried to climb aboard, only to be told by Walt that Claude would "spoil the scale" of the pony-sized coach with his 6' 6" height.

Joe Fowler suggested to Walt that they could keep the stagecoaches, but perhaps stop having guests ride on the top. But Walt exclaimed, "Oh, Joe, if we don't have the people on top of the coaches, it's no show. Besides the [darn] horses are gettin' their heads off. Let's discontinue it and have the mule ride."

They did continue to have the pack mule ride for years, despite the Bob Gurr animated sheep incident we've already talked about. But eventually it, too, was deemed too much of a liability and the mules retired from their daily treks through Nature's Wonderland in 1973.

I wish I could say that that was the end of the flawed Frontierland, but we can't forget the blatant hazards of the Frontierland Shootin' Gallery. This target shooting attraction replaced the miniature horse corral in 1957, complete with a fictional town of Boot Hill for guests to sight down the barrel of their guns. But unlike today where infrared beams trigger animation for expert shots, the original iteration of this attraction featured actual lead pellets. The pellets would chip away at the paint so badly that maintenance spent hours every night repainting the town of

Boot Hill. It wasn't until 1985 that they finally gave up the ghost and converted to the infrared system.

I find that a little incredible, truly. That Disney spent not years, but *decades* painstakingly repainting an entire miniature old west town every night. That no one thought of an easier way sooner, even if technology hadn't yet evolved enough to have what we have today.

But they were used to painting it. Doing thousands of little touch-ups, everyday, for 28 years.

Sometimes it's hard to see the flaw in our personal patterns until we step away from them.

We get caught up in our ruts, in our routines, so much so that we don't even consider any other way.

Speaking of ruts, I was talking to my *Distory* podcast cohost the other day about how the wagon wheel ruts from the Oregon Trail still exist in Eastern Oregon. You can go on out to the National Historic Oregon Trail Interpretive Center, walk down a (sometimes sweltering) pathway into the valley and see the two lines framed by sagebrush leading towards the Blue Mountains in the distance. The lines were made by thousands of Conestoga wagons, just like the ones in Disneyland, filled with the hopes and dreams of pioneers longing for a better life.

For change.

For some, the journey must have felt like a mistake at times. It was an arduous trip, fraught with danger and uncertainty. Some abandoned all their possessions in the middle of nowhere just to make it over a stubbornly steep hill. Some buried loved ones along the way as disease and starvation took them, one by one. Some got lost, felt hopeless, and wondered if they would ever get to where they needed to be.

When put in the context of what the Old West was actually like, Disneyland's early Frontierland captured that spirit, and then some. Disney struggled. They built museums that no one cared about. Had animals that they had to give up on. And had times when what was planned became too dangerous, and they had to reroute and go in another direction.

But through all the growing pains, Frontierland holds another part of the pioneering spirit as well: it never gave up.

Disney learned from every trip and fall. They took failed attractions and turned them into new ones, and then updated those as the years went by so they wouldn't get stale. They found new, inventive ways of bringing people an immersive experience, all the while decreasing the labor needed to maintain it. And Walt learned to let go of the vision he had for his Old West town full of stagecoaches and wagons and trade it for something that served guests in a better (safer) way.

I sometimes wonder what would have happened if Disney hadn't changed a thing about the original Frontierland. If they had dug in their heels and refused to acknowledge the flaws and the failures. Or I consider the alternative, if they had abandoned the Frontierland concept full stop when it seemed like nothing was working out as they had planned.

They could have done what some of the pioneers did, the ones we don't usually talk about with reverence and awe. The ones who gave up along the way, deeming the path ahead too hard, too scary.

Those pioneers knew there was a land ahead with abundance and plenty, but they settled for building houses out of sod in the barren land where their hope died. The ones who refused to take another step, and instead made a home where their heart broke.

Sometimes we make mistakes, and we give up in the middle of the prairie. We decide the journey isn't worth the pain. The healing isn't worth the hurt. The mistakes can't be unmade. And we build ourselves a house out of the sod of our poor choices, believing we deserve to live in them forever.

But if Disney *had* given up on Frontierland, abandoned the pioneering spirit that perseveres through hard times, it wouldn't be a reminder to us today that our mistakes are not definitive. That they are not a tattoo we wear on our forehead or an anchor holding us down.

No, they are an invitation to *persevere*. To grow. To reinvent ourselves with the knowledge of who we never want to be again.

It's never too late to pack your wagon and move toward greener pastures, even if it feels like you don't deserve them.

I assure you, you do.

You deserve to live in a land of Rainbow Caverns and Big Thunders.

You can let go of the overturned stagecoaches of your past. To depart from the rut of remembering all the ways you failed.

Because today is the day you get to decide to travel in a new direction.

The next time you step into Frontierland, let it be a place that surrounds you with the hope of rising from the ashes of past failures. Let it gift you with the "faith, courage, and ingenuity of the pioneers who blazed the trails across America," as its dedication plaque originally read.

Let yourself let go of what was and find a new frontier.

Because it's never too late to chase the horizon, even if the sun has set on the dreams you used to have.

Permission To Fly

He missed out on his childhood

put to work holding up his dad's dreams and expectations

a little boy crying in a cold stairwell

having slipped down a flight of icy stairs

placing the newspapers that his dad took credit for delivering.

That's the boy who didn't want to grow up.

Later, all his dreams were coming true

he hit the big-time

creating a lucky rabbit that captured attention.

But a ruthless man who wanted his luck stole it from under him

luring all his artists and friends away behind his back

the betrayal stung

and he worked feverishly to save what he had built

working in secret

as the Judas's still lingered in his space.

That's the boy who didn't want to grow up.

Still later, people who created alongside him called him unfair.

They claimed he played favorites

they didn't like how they were treated

so those he called friends walked out instead of conversing

and his trust was shattered.

A few came back

but the walls he built were stalwart and strong

and most were held on the outside of his inner thoughts

never the same as it was before.

That's the boy who didn't want to grow up.

So he immersed himself in pixie dust and pirates,

wanting to believe

that there could be a place where shadows could be disconnected

and the weight of responsibility could be left behind.

That little boy who didn't want to grow up

created a Neverland for himself in ink and paint

and then brought it to life

where he could sit in a pirate galleon

and look down on the world he wished

had been his from the beginning.

Now we do the same

the ones who are given the permission to fly

and think happy thoughts

and remember what it was like

before we grew up.

14

THE OPEN DRAWBRIDGE

In another life, I wore a barista's apron instead of Mickey ears for a living.

I worked at Seattle's Best Coffee in downtown Seattle's Pioneer Square, a place that held a confusing blend of tourists and corporate business clientele by day and clubbing/unhoused residents by night. My husband Eliot and I, newly married, lived on the same block as my place of employment, and I have vivid memories of him calling the police as I watched in horror from our fifth-story window as one man beat another with a 2x4 at midnight.

Needless to say, it was a colorful place to live and work.

While weekdays were filled with pulling shots by hand the old-fashioned way and memorizing hundreds of regular customer drink orders so they wouldn't roll their eyes when you asked what you could get for them, weekends were scarily quiet in the business district, often only seeing a handful of people during my entire 8-hour shift.

It was on such a day when it happened.

I was restocking the Nanaimo bars in the display case and chatting with my female coworker (we'll call her Angie for our purposes here) as our male coworker (let's call him Sam) was doing dishes in the back.

Time passed excruciatingly slowly as it did most Saturdays. We watched the occasional tourist pass by the glass windows trying to find the nearby Underground Tour. We did a deep clean of everything in the cafe, including fridges and cabinets speckled with spilled milk and syrups. And we looked on in horror as a gentleman sprinkled cocoa powder from our condiment bar on a table and then licked it off, again and again.

As Angie and I debated about who would disinfect the table after he eventually left, I realized Sam had been doing the dishes for a long time. When I went back to investigate, the sinks were still full and Sam was nowhere to be found. I informed Angie of the situation, and she suggested I check the employee restroom, located within the labyrinth of our highrise building through a door in the back of our storage room.

After winding my way down to the door of the restroom, I knocked and asked Sam if he was okay. No answer. I knocked again, more insistent, but still Sam was silent. I was scared that something had happened to him, so I warned Sam I was coming in as I tried the handle, which, to my surprise, opened with no resistance.

What I found shocked me.

Sam's apron was on the floor like he had been raptured and left only his barista career behind.

Puzzled, I picked it up and hurried back to Angie, shoving the apron at her and babbling about Sam being gone. She looked puzzled for a moment, and then her eyes widened.

"We should check his cash register," she said.

I was frozen in disbelief.

Sam was someone I'd trained as a barista for over a month. We spent hours together joking and having fun. No way would he do something like that.

Right?

But he did. Sam had cleaned out over $300 from his register when Angie and I were busy elsewhere, and never came back.

We of course filed a police report and managed the situation, but something changed in me that day. Because I had always been so trusting, and never had I even considered that someone I knew would do something like that.

I saw my coworkers a little differently after that.

And I wonder if that's how the Red Wagon Inn Disneylanders (early nomenclature for Cast Members) felt back in 1960, as well. Because that's when the very first holdup in Disneyland history occurred in the park.

According to 25-year-old cashier Robert Lowry, he was taking a $10,000 deposit to the bank on Main Street U.S.A. when a bandit came up behind him, pressed an object into his back, and ordered him into a restroom backstage. The bandit then took the bag containing the money and commanded Lowry to stay put as he made his escape.

Lowry claimed he never saw the man. But he did, because the man who had stolen the deposit was the same one who looked back at him in the mirror every day.

When the Anaheim police started questioning Lowry, he had a hard time keeping his story straight. Sometimes he said the bandit had a gun, other times a knife. Sometimes he threatened Lowry's person, sometimes his family. The police grew wary, as his testimony "just didn't jibe." They finally made Lowry take a lie detector test, and that's when he cracked and admitted he knew where the cash was.

Leading them back to Disneyland, Lowry revealed the deposit was safe and sound, stored in several boxes in the linen closet of the Red Wagon Inn. He was charged with grand theft, and, to the best of my knowledge, lost his access to the Happiest Place on Earth.

Sam and Robert weren't who they pretended to be. They both presented themselves as innocent, trustworthy people who would do the right thing, and then they took advantage of people's trust for their own benefit.

Our own sense of justice wants to see these people pay for their crimes. They took something that wasn't theirs. They betrayed those who trusted them. They lied about who they were. And while it doesn't always involve large sums of cash as a crime, the sad truth is, we have people that do that to *us* more often than we may want to admit.

People who manipulate our feelings to get what they want or make themselves feel important.

People who wear masks that look so real we can't tell the difference until we're finding aprons on the floor of our hearts, wondering how we didn't see the signs sooner.

We feel stupid that we trusted. Believed what they told us. Cared about their well-being. Gave pieces of ourselves to them that they didn't tend or nurture, but instead used them as stepping stones for achieving their own desires.

After feeling betrayed, you start to second-guess yourself. You wonder if the world has inverted its colors and you were just too naive to tell. What if what you thought was red was actually green? Or vibrant yellows were always hiding black underneath? Or what you thought was love was just a person who saw you as someone they could easily use?

You start to question, to wonder if anyone can be trusted at all. You begin to build walls as high as the castle's tallest spire because no one is safe anymore. Silence is better than words that might be lies. Independence is better than pain.

But the more time you spend in the reality of your walled-off heart, the more out of reach you become. Your gate gets rusty. You can't move. Can't breathe.

And you can't love anyone else, because that would mean you have to open yourself up to the possibility that someone may take what's good about you and run off with it again, leaving you with broken windows that you have no choice but to replace with more bricks.

So how do we deal with the Sams and Roberts in our world? Do we give up loving anyone ever again because we know it will hurt?

While I think it's wise to be cautious and protective of our hearts, knowing that not everyone has earned the privilege of accessing them, raising the castle drawbridge and permanently shutting out the world isn't the answer. Because while you limit the access of those who would do you harm, you also keep out all of the lovely humans who deserve a chance to step inside and sit with you in your courtyard. People who may be not only quality companions but who need your peace and security, as well.

Disneyland's Sleeping Beauty Castle has only had its drawbridge raised twice in Disney history: Once for the park's opening ceremonies in 1955, and again in 1983 when New Fantasyland was premiered to the public. I remember hearing Tony Baxter say that they weren't sure the mechanism to operate the bridge would actually work after sitting for almost 30 years, and they were pleasantly surprised when it did.

But even though Disney could potentially secure the castle, keeping guests out of Fantasyland, it hasn't been closed since. In fact, it's pretty well permanently cemented & bolted down, allowing us to walk through its open portcullis again and again as many times as we like.

It chooses to stay open, even though it could close itself off.

And we need to choose that, too.

Because, at the end of the day, the risk of loving people is always better than sitting safely by yourself in your castle turret, wondering why you feel so alone.

It's a Small World After All

Smiling faces from a thousand different places

different opinions

opposing beliefs

I want to believe it is a small world after all

but how do we reconcile the chasm between us

when some take without giving

and hurt more than help

when a few of those smiling faces hide fangs

looking for an easy meal

looking for a gullible soul who believes that people are good on the inside

they are who the rotten seek first

the gold and white

Like Mary Blair chose for her final scene

those who are unspoiled

who haven't yet been hurt beyond healing

or stepped on by those who think they don't matter

we all exist together in this world

the broken and the breakers

the question is

which one will you be?

15

ANIMATING FORCES

Every good story has a villain, and Disney's stories are no exception.

As I've studied the animators who created all these Disney characters, I have found their different approaches to crafting the villains we know and love fascinating, because none of their creative processes were the same.

Let's take a look at three artists for context, and the characters they animated, starting with Bill Tytla.

Volodymyr Peter Tytla, otherwise known as Bill, was a Ukrainian-American animator who was one of the first people at Disney Studios to create characters that evoked an emotional connection with the audience. Animation had begun as just a silly, slapstick piece of nonsense before the feature presentation; it was never considered serious and certainly not as emotionally compelling as "real" films. But Walt Disney had a vision, a passion for creating convincing characters that you wanted to cheer for, or cry for, or both. And Bill was one of those people who could do just that.

One of Bill Tytla's first major assignments at Walt Disney Studios was Grumpy in *Snow White*. Perhaps one of the loveliest scenes in the movie is one in which Snow White kisses Grumpy's head, and as he walks away, his gruff demeanor slowly melts away as the realization that he is loved reaches his heart. While all of this takes place in a short span of a few frames, the impact of this moment, created by an animated character, ripples throughout the movie, as the hand-drawn personalities connect in a profound way with our humanity and our desire to be loved and accepted for who we are.

But Bill didn't only animate loveable characters. In fact, he is likely more well-known for his dastardly villains than anything else. Bill was the one who brought Chernabog to life in *Fantasia*'s "*Night on Bald Mountain*" sequence, as well as creating the large and lumbering giant in the 1938 short *Brave Little Tailor*, a character who became the industry standard for how giants were portrayed. And then there was one of the most evil and repulsive villains of all, the child-exploiting Stromboli from *Pinocchio*. Bill didn't just draw the characters he created, he *became* them. As animators Frank Thomas and Ollie Johnston put it, "Everything was 'feelings' with Bill. Whatever he animated had the inner feelings of his characters expressed through very strong acting. He did not just get inside Stromboli, he was Stromboli and he lived that part."

It was said of Bill that in order to access what he needed to create these characters, he had to live in their heads, so to speak, and think like they would think. When asked about his creation of Chernabog, Bill explained, "I imagined that I was as big as a mountain and made of rock, and yet I was feeling and moving." His sketches portray the same sentiment of internal struggle as Bill was aggressive with his drawing, often making lines so rough that they would rip through the paper. I think

Donald Graham put it perfectly when he said of Bill in a 1937 studio art class, "It is obvious that he does not animate forms, but forces."

Not all Disney villains were made with such interiority, however. Marc Davis, for example, looked more outward than inward for his inspiration for the character of Cruella de Vil. Though Ken Anderson and Bill Peet also worked on early concepts for this character, it was Marc who became her keyframe animator. He retained the mink coat present in the original 1956 novel by Dodie Smith, but Marc would add an element of cruelty and devilishness by giving the iconic coat it's bright red inner lining. Cruella's personality was inspired by someone Marc knew in real life who was slender, tall and talked constantly, making it difficult for anyone else to get a word in edgewise. Betty Lou Gerson also made her way into the film as more than just the voice of Cruella, as Marc noticed her larger-than-life persona and how she was always in motion, like a shark looking for its prey (among other qualities, we'll get into that later).

But interestingly enough, Marc did not use any of the live-action reference footage Disney had captured of actress Mary Wickes much when it came to animating Cruella. His reasoning was that he wanted the character to move in a way that seemed unnatural and displeasing to the eye, emphasizing the idea that Cruella made her own way in the world and didn't care about anyone's opinion but her own. All of these elements together turned Cruella into a villain that was easy to hate (well, that and her love of skinning puppies for fur coats).

Our third animator is one who some would say is a bit of a villain himself, Milt Kahl. He once told Marc his Medusa character would "wipe [his] Cruella off the screen" (which gives you a little insight into what he thought of himself and his work). Though Milt was a brilliant artist who brought us several villains like Shere Khan and Mad Madam Mim, he stated that his favorite character to animate was one based on someone he knew all too well: his ex-wife.

Arguably one of the most heartless characters of all of Disney animation, Medusa from *The Rescuers* was a caricature of Phyllis Bounds, Walt Disney's niece and second wife to Milt. Phyllis was a heavy-drinking, chain-smoking, hard-living woman who wasn't afraid to share her opinions. She had married and divorced four times, with each husband having some association with Disney Studios. Her first husband was a gas station attendant there before she divorced him and moved on to having an affair with a married man, noted photographer George Hurrell, who would then divorce his wife and marry Phyllis. They had three kids before getting divorced. Phyllis then went on to marry Disney animator David Detiege in 1958. When that didn't last, she was eventually fixed up (by Marc and Alice Davis) with Milt Kahl, and the two tied the knot and lived a contentious married life for just shy of ten years before calling it quits.

Milt was known to have a cruel streak and a fiery temper, and he was also extremely competitive with Phyllis. When she decided to learn a new skill like tap dancing or how to play the piano, he decided he would do it too–and then worked hard to be better at it than she was. Phyllis wasn't particularly easy to live with either, as she drank heavily, much to Milt's displeasure. As animator and director Richard Williams put it, "She talked like a producer and tucked the alcohol away."

As their marriage was grinding to a halt, Milt was clearly fed up with the "aging sexpot attitude" of his wife and decided to take his frustration out in character form. From her fake eyelashes to her iconic boots, Phyllis Bounds became his character Medusa, with all her flaws on display for the world to see. Milt translated his soon-to-be-ex-wife's cartoonish personality into Medusa's characteristic flamboyance in *The Rescuers*.

Milt was finding a way to channel his anger and pain from his broken relationship into something worthwhile.

I wonder if we can do the same.

We encounter our own villains in our lives, though some don't see themselves as such. And along the way, wounds start to appear from our encounters with each one. Some heal with time, and some refuse to do so, insisting on coming back to visit and being a part of our story.

But the villains that caused the pain? We want them to care that they caused it, to see what pain they inflicted. While not all of us can paint our character on the big screen to illustrate our anger and frustration, we still hope that one day they will see what they did and be sorry for it.

But that's the thing about villains: they rarely apologize. And waiting for it? That is what can turn *you* into a villain, too.

We like to pack up our wounds and close them away in a suitcase where we don't have to look at them too closely, but then we spend a lifetime carrying them around from place to place. They grow heavier over time as we add more and more hurt from people we trust, and before long, we can't pick up the suitcase at all. Instead, we get stuck with it, shouting at people who walk by us so freely, angry and bitter about the weight of the pain others have handed us. They then, in turn, are hurt by our words, adding them to their collection in their own suitcases, and on and on it goes till all of us are simply yelling at each other while holding our overloaded suitcases, when really all we are is just terribly, terribly hurt.

But we don't have to choose to put all of our wounds in a suitcase. Instead, we can acknowledge that the villains are there because they are a necessary part of our story.

Every good story has a villain. A person who tries to drag you down and keep you believing that your life is less valuable than theirs, or that you don't deserve a happy ending.

No doubt, it would be much easier to skip the whole evil villain part and get on to the happily-ever-after. But villains exist in our world because they grow us into who we need to be. They make us stronger because we have to fight, have to struggle to overcome, and in doing so we pick up hope to hand to others when they are facing their own enemies. We hand others in pain the keys to unlock their suitcases and give them permission to unpack every wound inflicted by someone who didn't care for them as they should have.

Like it or not, villains push us onto paths we wouldn't have bothered treading without their presence.

Villains take us to dark places so that we can truly appreciate the light.

Bill Tytla eventually got tired of animating dark, moody villains for Disney studios, and was ready to spend his days on something more positive. He was worn out from being typecast as the evil villain. He wanted more. So one day he asked for a lighter assignment and was put on the team producing a new film. He then spent his days embodying joy and light as he analyzed his own son Peter's mannerisms and transformed them into a character who was rejected and yet still loved; a tiny baby elephant named Dumbo.

Facing Villains

Picking up the pieces of the life I used to have

I packed my meager possessions in a box

objects that had defined a chapter of my life

but now held memories I wanted to forget.

I walked out the door in bewilderment

and stepping down the crumbling stairs I thought of the irony

that falling apart should happen so pervasively.

As I slammed my car door

it felt like a period at the end of a sentence that had run on too long

and I cried.

I thought of all the people who had faced villains before

princesses who were poisoned, and captured, and diminished

fake kings who stole from the poor to feed the rich

and greedy sheriffs who took more than their fair share.

I thought of other women

other people who had also been told

what they did wasn't important

who were weighed down with purpose

and struggled to see it come to fruition

because no one took the time to see them

despite their artistry

despite their creativity.

It's all just a reminder that

villains come in all shapes and sizes.

Some don't realize their villainy,

but their destruction is tangible even if their awareness is not.

We can't make them more aware

but we can do better

we can love more

by seeing those around us as we were never seen

and not letting our bitterness

turn us into the villain

in someone else's story.

Unfurling The Sails

She was just a guest posing for a picture

aboard a tuna sandwich pirate ship in a theme park

and yet I see myself there

holding on loosely to the wheel

not really steering the ship

as the wind has blown me in a direction

I never intended to go.

I can adjust my sails

sure

I have in the past, over and over,

when the tide was not in my favor

but for now, I just pause and survey

where do I make land

when the port has washed away?

I breathe

grip the wheel one last time

feel the grain of the wood under my tired hands

and finally start to accept

that the harder I hold on fighting against the current

the more splinters I will get in my palms

so let I go

unfurl my sails

and let the wind move me where it will

because I can have an adventure anywhere I go

but not if I don't first surrender

the one that wasn't mine to keep.

16

WHEN NOTHING IS GOING RIGHT

The night before Disneyland opened, everything was chaos.

Main Street wasn't yet paved, its trolley track bones exposed as the asphalt had yet to be poured around them. Tomorrowland lacked the moving walkways that were supposed to be a main feature of the World of Tomorrow, and instead, the entire land was a world of disappointing compromises and malfunctioning equipment.

The ABC television crew fought with the construction workers for space as one group of people tried to set up for the world's largest live broadcast while the other struggled to make something that looked broadcast-worthy. The consequences of worker strikes, labor union disputes, and impossible construction timelines had started to rear their ugly head, and crews worked non-stop painting, planting, and finishing projects that should have been done months before.

And Walt Disney? Well, he was working too.

Navigating his way around Disneyland by bike, he would move from worksite to worksite, checking on progress and, no doubt, internally wishing he could wave a magic wand and have it all completed in time for his network-imposed broadcast deadline. He spent time in the "squid room" of the *20,000 Leagues Under the Sea* exhibition, desperately pitching in to help finish the somewhat last-minute display of props from the movie of the same name. On a night when Walt Disney should have been preparing for the launch of his new park, he was instead in his work clothes spray-painting an underwater mural behind Bob Mattey's rubber squid, the one that guests would later spy through a circular window in Captain Nemo's salon.

Even after hours of painting, it was clear that the hallways and furniture would not be assembled in time for the exhibit to open the next day. Walt moved around the park, hurrying the painting of the carrousel along and probably shaking his head at the half-painted pirate ship, the centerpiece of Fantasyland still missing all of its rigging and sails. Well after midnight, Walt eventually found his way to Main Street U.S.A. with Ken Anderson in tow, both of them sitting down on a curb with their feet in the dust, their first break of the day.

And that's when someone told them Mr. Toad had no power because someone had cut the wires to the attraction.

Ken said to Walt, "Don't worry, I'll take care of it," and got up to investigate the problem, leaving Walt to contemplate his reality that nothing seemed to be going right.

I think we've all felt like Walt on that curb.

I know I have.

There are times when it feels like life keeps happening, one unprecedented event after another. You bob and weave and learn and grow and still you can't escape the chaos. You start to laugh when another thing falls apart, or breaks, or ends. Because of course, it would.

All of it can make you want to sit on the curb, maybe forever. Because down there, things can't get worse. You're already defeated. Sunk so low you might as well become one with the dust on Main Street.

But Main Street didn't stay dusty.

That place where Walt sat, his feet covered in the dirt of his apparent failure, *that* is now a path toward happiness for millions every year. It's a road showing the way forward for those who need to step into a new story, reminding them that happily ever after is possible as long as you don't give up and sit on the curb.

Maybe Walt knew that, and that's what made him get up. Knowing that even in failure, there was hope.

Disneyland's opening day was, in fact, a tremendous failure by all accounts. Too many people without adequate food or water. Crushes of crowds with endless broken rides. A gas leak threatened to take out Tomorrowland, freshly-poured asphalt captured women's heels, and the *Mark Twain* almost sank with 508 souls aboard (it was only in eight feet of water though, so they would have likely been okay). The *Dateline: Disneyland* live television broadcast was so chaotic that many times the commentators didn't even talk about what was actually being shown on the screen. Ronald Regan, co-host of the broadcast, had to scale an eight-foot fence in Frontierland to make his appearance on time. Even Walt Disney was seen running with toilet paper to restock a bathroom that had run out of the necessity.

But they did it. They opened Disneyland.

Was it perfect? Hardly.

But nothing is, really.

If Walt hadn't had a disastrous opening of Disneyland, he might not have felt compelled to pour millions of dollars into improving the park, "plussing" attractions and lands in the years to come. It was that drive to improve, to keep changing the living film that was Disneyland that kept curious guests returning year after year to see what Mr. Disney was up to. Where most amusement parks floundered after their first few years, Disneyland thrived.

All because Walt had sat on that curb in the dust, looking around at a whole lot of failure.

If you're sitting on your own curb right now wondering if it's worth getting back up, remember that the chaos is temporary, and it's leading somewhere. No moment of heartbreak or hurt is ever wasted, it's just writing a story you get to share with others later on when you find them sitting in the dust.

Sometimes they may need to just be there awhile, taking in the view from the curb, and figuring out where to go from here.

And it's okay if you need to do that, too.

But don't let this one moment in time define all the rest of your moments hereafter. There's more for you than chaos and failure and endless heartache—I promise.

And someday when you've made it to the end of the street, the view looking back will be the most breathtaking sight you'll ever see, not because it was perfect, but because it was imperfectly assembled from all of your mistakes and flaws.

Disneyland's story is beautifully imperfect.

And it's okay if yours is, too.

The Fake Lampposts

The lampposts on Main Street U.S.A. are real, but also fake.

Maybe we are that way, too.

The lampposts once were entirely real,

illuminating the streets of metropolitan thoroughfares like Baltimore, Philadelphia, and St. Louis.

People walked in and out of their circles of light, on their way to this place or that.

They were functional.

Needed to light up dark places and chase criminals into the shadows.

Fast forward 160 years, and electricity was all the rage.

The gas lamps that had so faithfully served were no longer needed,

so they were removed, discarded.

But some—a few lucky ones—ended up at Disneyland, purchased for a mere $.08 per pound.

They illuminated sidewalks once more, albeit on a street with pony-sized buildings and storybook-tinted dreams.

And again, people walked in and out of their circles of light.

Strings of lights were installed on the buildings of Main Street for Christmas, though, and lingered after because Walt liked the look.

The gas lamps stayed, but ceased to cast circles of light.

Then, disaster.

Water under pressure wore away the tired metal.

The lampposts had served, but not all of them could go on.

They were replaced with fiberglass, sturdy and sure.

But fake.

Except, not.

They hold the shape and the memories of what came before, even if they are not what they once were.

And clinging on to each lamppost are layers of paint, added to cover the change.

Some equate the layers with falsity, hiding the truth of the matter.

But the layers are actually protection, coupled with their history of previous illuminated nights at Disneyland.

We wear such layers.

People often see the outer part, the touched-up layer that happily shines and shows no imperfections for them to stop and ponder. Yet, underneath, we have carefully tucked away the pieces of us that we think people will not want to know.

Sometimes we aren't at all who we used to be, as fiberglass as they come.

And there's a reason for that.

The lampposts have a story, one that most will never fully understand. They could easily be called "fake."

People could call us "fake," too.

But they don't see all our layers.

Those who do, who pause in the circle of light and look closer, they are the ones we create light for. They are the ones we invite to tap gently, to hear the truth of what we've been through, hoping they will love us all the more despite our past.

Or maybe because of it.

The lampposts on Main Street are fake.

But not.

Finding #42

The hatbox ghost was a mistake.

He materialized on the right side of the attic in 1969

set in place for the cast member previews

a grand finale to an attic scene that slowly grew more grim

as your doom buggy wove through a maze of discarded life debris

and ghost skulls popping out of hatboxes to say hello.

All of it held ominous foreshadowing

accompanied by a steady heartbeat

fluttering bats

and strings of cobwebs that found your skin in the dark.

Then you saw her

a bride so frightening

you turned to race to the window

but before you made your escape

there he was, on the right

hand shaking on his cane

face appearing then disappearing into his hatbox

again and again

except... it didn't always disappear.

Sometimes it remained light when it should have been dark

or never illuminated at all

showing his face when it should have been absent

it was a disappointment

a failure of illusion

so they pulled figure #42 out of his place, and tried to fix him

but no matter how they tried to make him what they wanted him to be

they eventually surrendered hope

gave up

moved the bride to his former spot

and #42 became simply "omitted" on paper.

Over time guests began to question their memory

had he ever actually existed

had they only made him up in their minds

wanting him to be real

stories and songs highlighted his presence and yet he was illusive

a mistake that couldn't be remedied

except by time

because one day the mold that had formed him was pulled out

his head held in the hands of those who saw more than failure

and they found a way forward

giving the hatbox ghost

a second chance to see and be seen.

And so today that failed apparition

is known as #42 again

and his face disappears and reappears, grinning at us in the darkness

happy to be back where he was always meant to be.

He simply needed someone who wouldn't give up on him

who didn't see him as a mistake

but rather a person in progress

just like us.

A New Friend

It was too scary.

It frightened children and adults alike

with phantom strings in the dark that stroked faces of passing guests

and a witch that was everywhere, all at once

offering no escape, only apples.

Parents wrote letters

because Snow White was supposed to be a cute love story

that's what people remembered from the movie

when they climbed aboard wooden mine cars emblazoned with dwarf
names.

"Snow White and Her Adventures"

that was the expectation

but suddenly they were in a dungeon

then a dark forest

with flying bats and snapping crocodiles

phantom arms reached out to ensnare and entrap

and a cackling voice foreshadowed a less-than-happy ending

with Snow White nowhere in sight.

Walt heard the complaints

but simply said, "We all have to learn that life is scary sometimes."

So they tacked up a warning

(that most people missed)

and fear remained a staple of Fantasyland

reminding us that we can overcome scary things.

We can survive people who are rotten on the inside

and terrifying situations we didn't expect.

And somewhere along the way

Fear becomes a new friend

that we make space for

because Walt was right.

It's a part of life

and sometimes it chases us

toward an ending we didn't anticipate

but needed in the end

more than the perfectly happy one.

17

WHERE WE ALL BEGIN

As Walt looked over the massive patch of exposed dirt, fear eclipsed his dream.

The money was half-gone for the wild idea of building a theme park in the middle of a dusty orange grove, and yet nothing was there.

No storybook castles.

No spinning carrousels.

No soaring elephants.

Atop a makeshift wooden observatory tower in the middle of what was supposed to be Disneyland, Walt Disney stood with tears in his eyes as reality hit home. He spoke scary words to Harper Goff that day, ones that likely felt like a nail in a coffin for his hopes of building a magical kingdom for people to enjoy. With great sadness, Walt said, "I have the money half spent, and nothing to show for it. Nothing."

And it was true. They had moved 350,000 cubic yards of dirt and countless orange, walnut, and eucalyptus trees, and laid thousands of feet of sewer, gas, and water infrastructure below ground. But on the surface, not a single building was in sight.

Beginnings are hard.

They often make us want to give up before we've even truly begun.

Blank pages, piles of dirt, a dream we've held close to the vest but are hesitant to release, all of these things are terrifying because they look like nothing.

But can you imagine if Walt stood on that tower that day and said, "Forget it" when Disneyland looked like nothing?

Eventually, money was found to finance the park, between making a deal with ABC for a television show featuring the lands of Disneyland to Walt himself selling a beloved Smoke Tree Ranch property and also borrowing against his life insurance. Cuts were made for time and resources, and creative penny-pinching solutions were thought up to keep moving forward.

Grass that had turned brown under the hot California sun was spray-painted green to give the illusion of lush landscaping in lieu of new sod. Weeds were given Latin name signs in the hopes of passing them off as legitimately planned foliage. Tomorrowland was almost canceled altogether in September of 1954 for lack of time and resources but was thankfully put back on the table, financially propped up by corporate sponsors like Monsanto, Kaiser Aluminum, Richfield Oil, and Crane Plumbing (though, to be fair, what opened in 1955 was far from what Walt had hoped for the land. Drastic improvements were made in 1956 and beyond to bring it up to Disney standards for both show and detail).

There were other cuts, too, when it came to creating Disneyland. Radical methods of construction were employed to meet the one-year deadline, a goal that, to us, seems unfathomable today.

Landscaper Bill Evans said Disneyland was made with "a maximum of arm waving and a minimum of drawings," and in many cases that was true. The vehicles for Mr. Toad's Wild Ride were replicated from an Arrow Development prototype built from studio artist Bruce Bushman's sketch, skipping the blueprints altogether. The river path for the Jungle Cruise was created by Harper Goff by simply taking a stick and tracing one side of the river in the dirt, then walking 10-15 feet and tracing the other side. They didn't even have a plan for the river at all until they got to the construction bid stage and a contractor demanded it.

One of my favorite captured moments from this era's chaotic design process is a photo of Ken Anderson and Ralph Hulett working on an early plan for the "Peter Pan Fly Through" ride, as it was first going to be called. Ken Anderson is holding up a piece of Neverland concept art while Ralph is on the floor atop a sketch of ride layout, using a magic marker to sketch the ride's path through the story of the boy who refused to grow up.

I find it so fascinating because it's not one of the perfectly posed pictures we usually see of a group of Imagineers standing around a model and pointing, or pretending to paint something long past finished. It's not an artist sketching something for the camera. It's literally Ralph Hulett on his hands and knees on a giant plan for the attraction, surrounded by miscellaneous artwork from other films and rides, trying to map out a story to transport guests to Neverland. (Okay, so there *might* be a little bit of posing here based on the angles and the fact that Ralph is drawing something he already drew, but you get the idea).

These artists who created Disneyland didn't really know what they were doing–in a sense. They were filmmakers creating a concept that had never been done before, pioneering in every sense of the word. They didn't do what everyone else was doing, or even in the expected way of getting it done. But get it done they did, as they built all of Disneyland in just one year.

Sometimes we can be on our hands and knees pouring our heart and soul into something new, surrounded by all that's come before, and wondering if it's worth it. Wondering if it will work, especially when it's so different. But it's the most unique challenges that we pursue that make the biggest difference.

If your plans feel like they are just a giant map on a cluttered floor (or if all you have is a stick sketching in the dirt), keep going. Because the most magical and unique ideas in the world all started with someone deciding they were worthwhile to get down on the floor and sketch.

Embrace Change

The Water is Still Now

The water is still now

except for some ripples

caused by the most popular ducks in the world.

It was once a vast waterway

a cruise

for Tomorrowland Boats

which became Phantom ones

the first Disney ride to close

but not forever

as Motorboats arrived

delighting children

captained behind the wheel

but years passed

and interest waned

and despite travels to Gummi Glen

the boats were doomed

hope left when the tracks departed

and the water was still.

It was given a new name

Fantasia Gardens

and the boats were just a memory.

We too move from Phantom to Motor to Fantasia

growing and adapting and changing

until we slow down our pace

taking our time as our joints creak

and our memories take us on past adventures

the motorboat cruises we made yesterday become our remember whens

phantoms of what used to be

still alive and well in our minds

we can't stop the boats from changing

but we can learn to accept their process

because it gives us the opportunity

to notice the ripples

the ducks make on the water.

18

THE DISAPPEARING ACT

They say you don't really miss something until it's gone, and I think that sentiment is never more true than when it comes to the Disney Parks benches.

Walt Disney was fond of benches. He dreamed up Disneyland, or so the story goes, sitting on one in Griffith Park. He watched his two daughters on the merry-go-round and wished for a place where parents and children could have fun together, and it got the wheels turning for what would eventually become Disneyland. (You can still visit that bench, by the way, as it sits in the Opera House in Town Square.)

There is an iconic photo of Walt sitting on a bench on Main Street, pausing amidst his perpetual motion to stop and appreciate the little turn-of-the-century town he had dreamed up. Sometimes when I see that photo, I wonder what was going through his mind. Was he observing people enjoying his park, as he was known to do from his firehouse apartment? Was he mentally cataloging all the things that needed fixing? Jotting down notes in his mind about people he needed to talk to? Or was he simply taking it all in, being fully present in the moment and just enjoying Main Street U.S.A.?

We seek benches in the Disney parks most often for resting our weary feet, but Walt's vision of them went further. He had visited places like the historic Tivoli Gardens in Denmark in 1951 and observed what aesthetically pleasing spaces and beautifully landscaped surroundings could do for the soul. Disneyland was a *park*, first and foremost, meant for enjoyment. And, for some, the most enjoyable act of all was sitting and taking in the atmosphere from the comfort of a good bench positioned in a pleasant location.

This past summer, I made my first visit to Tivoli Gardens with my family, and it was like walking into the concept art for early Disneyland. A pirate ship sat quietly in a tranquil pond. World's Fair-style lights graced the lampposts. A Matterhorn-themed wooden roller coaster delighted my family (and scared me with the operator sitting on the vehicle and working the brake by hand), and I was thrilled to sit perched atop a horse on an ancient two-story merry-go-round, watching the park spin and spin around me. We drove miniature cars on diminutive roads, observed trolley cars rolling through the thoroughfares, and marveled at a giant whale next to a lighthouse reminiscent of Monstro and the Storybook Land Canal Boats.

But mostly, I observed the slower pace. In Tivoli, there isn't as much rushing around as there is in the Disney parks. People aren't interested in accomplishing as much as they are enjoying. I saw families with blankets picnicking on grassy banks and others stretched out in the sun having an afternoon siesta. Small gardens and sculptures were woven into the fabric of the park, inviting you to slow down and relax. There were spaces for children to play while adults conversed, but also plenty of places for all to have fun together.

It was a place of restoration and joy, and I could all but taste the direct inspiration for Disneyland.

While Disneyland still has these places of rest tucked into its corners, sometimes I feel like it's become more of an afterthought in our fast-paced, gotta-do-it-all world. If you look back at early photos of Disneyland, it is absolutely *covered* in benches and chairs for people to sit and rest on. Fantasyland had pastel concrete benches surrounding the pond where the Chicken of the Sea pirate ship used to dock (not unlike the one Walt saw in Tivoli). Tomorrowland had more "space age" seating that resembled school desks with individual tables attached to each one. And Main Street U.S.A., though it does have quite a few benches still today, had even more back then.

Some of my favorite benches are those that can be found in Magic Kingdom's Fantasyland outside Merlin's Magic Shop. Tucked under the eaves of one of the entrances, they are quiet and unassuming, but they used to be quite the opposite. With intricate scrollwork, lattice bottoms, and a tiered trio of backs, they certainly look fanciful and whimsical, even despite their black paint job. But they used to be even more so.

If you travel a couple of thousand miles and a few dozen years back, these benches used to appear at a similar location in Disneyland Park in Anaheim. They were the perfect place for people to sit and rest and enjoy the view of the back side of Sleeping Beauty Castle (which takes its inspiration from Neuschwanstein Castle at the foot of the German Alps and was meant to actually be the *front* of the castle in early concepts, but that's a story for another day). These benches are identical to the ones we see now in Walt Disney World, although they weren't black back then. No, these Fantasyland benches screamed fantasy; they were painted in such an array of bright pastel colors that they would put an Easter egg to shame.

When, exactly, these benches moved, I can only hazard a guess (because Walt Disney World photos of this obscure nook are rare), but my best estimation of their cross-country trek was likely in the early 1980s. This was when Disneyland was in the throws of remodeling their Fantasyland and was no doubt looking to make more room in that very congested spot in the park, made even more cramped by the expansion's plans to pull the attraction facades forward to create larger queues. It would make sense if Disney was going through all the trouble of moving the carrousel back 12 feet to give the area more breathing room that they would also remove a few benches while they were at it. And, as we all know, Disney loves to repurpose and reuse anything and everything. So it's more than likely they shipped these Fantasyland benches to Florida where they had room for them, or the "blessing of size," as Walt put it.

But their absence is felt.

I sometimes try to linger in this courtyard behind the castle, enjoying its beauty when the light is low and the gold accents shift and glow as Walt meant them to. But between the strollers, constant traffic, and lack of benches, I often give up because I feel more anxious and in the way than relaxed. I usually surrender my post under the eaves of Merlin's and go find quieter spaces like the old loading dock for the Motor Boat Cruise or the benches under the Monorail tracks alongside the Matterhorn, which thankfully still exist.

Not all benches have been that lucky, though. It seems a growing trend since the days of Paul Pressler that benches slowly started disappearing, one by one. And if you visit the Magic Kingdom, virtually none of their rows of benches on Main Street U.S.A. or the hub remain (or the shade trees, for that matter). Epcot is the same way, with relaxing places to sit seemingly being phased out.

I can only speculate about why. Perhaps they do it for traffic flow. Maybe maintenance costs. Or maybe they want to encourage you to do all your sitting in a restaurant, or not sitting at all so you're doing more financially-beneficial activities like shopping and snacking on the go. I don't know the reason, for sure. But I do know one thing: I miss the benches.

But every time my feet hurt from lack of places to perch, or my weary mind wishes it could stop and people watch for a while, I think of how little we thought of those benches while we had them. We assumed they were a given. Like Fastpasses and Magical Express bus rides, we assumed they would be there forever, part of our Disney experience.

We took them for granted, as we too often do for the quiet supports in our lives.

And so when I see the empty places where benches used to dwell, I pause and think of what I am grateful for, what still exists even when so much else feels like it's been lost.

I may not have benches, but I still have quiet castle views.

I may not have Fastpasses, but I still have spins in a teacup and rides on a caterpillar.

I may not have millions, but I have a million moments of joy.

Maybe that's what Walt thought about on his bench.

Not about what he lacked, but what he had.

A wealth built of moments on benches, watching people invest in each other.

Ghosts of Disneyland Past

Sometimes I wonder what Disneyland would be like

if all of its past became its present.

If paper hats perched on heads again

and grinder monkeys danced on Main Street

if the pharmacy handed out vitamins and displayed leeches

or the miniature horses in their corral regained their magical view of the castle next door.

I wonder if people would still buy candles shaped like hamburgers

or climb into the shrubbery for pictures

or enjoy an afternoon of model boat racing in the castle moat.

I wonder what it would be like

to spot Walt in disguise

wearing a hat as no local would do at the time

standing in line with the rest of us

dreaming up plans for change.

I wonder how it would feel to hand over a dime for a ride in the
horse-drawn trolley

or eagerly await the opening of Edison Square

while sipping my coffee at Maxwell House on Main Street

watching the people come and go

in and out of this place that is both fantasy and reality.

Sometimes I think the ghosts of what used to be linger in this space

and that's why it feels so intangibly magical.

Disneyland holds the happy memories of millions

moments that no longer exist in the present

but that we get to revisit it again and again

every time we leave today

and enter the world of yesterday, tomorrow, and fantasy.

Being Stretched

I long to be as unbothered as the stretching room occupants

The ones we see when we first step into the chamber

with no windows and no doors

before the danger is revealed.

I remember what it felt like to be that way

before I knew what I know now

blissfully unaware of what was to come.

I wonder when Marc Davis sketched these characters meant to make us
laugh

what he thought of them, really.

If they resembled real life

how we pretend and present a version of ourselves we wish we were

but underneath the surface

we are sinking

standing on shaky ground and powder kegs

holding onto thorny reminders of our past

that we'd rather keep buried

and walking tightropes trying to please people

too late discovering that the danger of doing so

is far worse than we imagined.

We stretch and stretch and stretch ourselves

till we no longer resemble who we once were

and that's when the true peril is revealed

Not alligators and axes

but the shadow versions of ourselves that are the greatest threat of all.

Perhaps, though, the stretching room portraits are not unbothered

but quite the opposite.

Haunted by their mistakes

pained by their past.

Yet we don't have to be like them.

We don't have to let the ghosts of our former selves

follow us home forever.

Because sometimes being stretched

is what reveals something we needed to see all along

and once we've seen it

we can finally rest in peace.

In the Portrait Gallery

The changing portraits changed in the Haunted Mansion

and not just from one image to another.

Marc Davis created many that never graced the ghostly walls

ideas that were abandoned along the way.

In this lost portrait gallery

the Burning Miser found his fate

fruit & flowers decayed at a rapid rate

Henry VIII stood proudly beside a headless Anne

Rasputin's eyes looked into your soul

and Daphne became a tree (without Apollo in pursuit).

April to December had two more months

and X. Atencio's farm succumbed to the Dust Bowl.

Even the portraits on display now

often had more scenes meant to fit between the first and the last

six slides instead of the two we know

the result of indecision about how long guests would linger in the hall.

Some of us do linger, however

seeing them all, one by one

reflections of consequences and hidden agendas

stories of our mortality and the inevitability of loss over time.

If the portraits didn't change

imagine what would be lost

static images that told no story

pictures that didn't move you emotionally one way or another.

It's in their changing that we see more than one perspective

because we always think we know the complete picture

until it shifts

and shows us how limited we are in what we can truly see.

The more we watch the figures morph and shift

the more we realize that we are the ones that need to change

to see our lives in new ways

to see others that way, too

to make room for change in the portrait hall of our minds

because our story is more than our reflection in the mirror

and it's not December yet.

19

GO ANOTHER WAY

Once upon a time, the Haunted Mansion was going to be a dilapidated affair with the voice of Walt Disney guiding guests through the decaying structure in the bayou. The idea was the Mansion was "under construction," but the ghosts wouldn't let them finish the house. As a 1957 script told guests, "Every day we made a new attempt to repair the house, but in vain, for every morning the windows were broken...the furniture smashed... the shutters hanging by a single hinge, and even new coats of paint scratched and peeled off." Though planned to be a walking tour of 40 guests at a time, this version of the mansion did have a ride vehicle of sorts that looked like scaffolding, made of 2x4s with railings and wheels.

But then the 1964 New York World's Fair happened, and Disney's Imagineers at WED learned about the value of capacity. They subsequently developed the Omnimover technology, a system that would move over 2,600 guests into the boundless realm of the supernatural every hour. Thus the idea of a walkthrough attraction with an identical two-sided mansion dematerialized into the ether (except for the two stretching rooms, of course).

The moldy Mansion didn't work as planned, so Disney went another way.

Casey Jr. Circus Train was once going to talk to kids in the station, wishing them Happy Birthday and chit-chatting with them to make the attraction an interactive one. The circus train would have gone through a volcano on its journey, traveling around an area called Lilliputian Land with a boat ride intertwined with its tracks. This volcano is evident in the earliest public preview of Disneyland and continued to show up in the concept art for a good long while. But today there is no rumbling volcano, only a quiet cave and a mountain peak featuring Cinderella's castle.

The erupting volcano didn't work as planned, so Disney went another way.

Adventureland, originally called True Life Adventureland, was going to have a botanical garden where you could buy an exotic pet, plant, or bird and take it home as a souvenir. Walt Disney also wanted a live alligator pen in the queue for the Jungle Cruise, which showed up in the model of the attraction. Ruth Shellhorn, the landscape architect for Disneyland, noted it in her construction journal, "Disney had a wild idea about an alligator in a pen." This was likely an addition Walt wanted because of the recently opened California Alligator Farm in Buena Park across from Knotts Berry Farm. Baby alligators were added to the Jungle Cruise queue for a short while, but they had a tendency to escape and eat the park's resident baby ducks, so a new home was found for them, and the pen was dismantled.

The alligator pen didn't work as planned, so Disney went another way.

Walt Disney hadn't planned on there being any skeletons in the Ghostly Grotto section of Pirates of the Caribbean. The original concept was that you were supposed to see the crew's quarters, possibly with a hot meal on the table, and think, "Where did the pirates go? They clearly must have just been here!" and then you went into the city and found them. But all that changed after Walt passed away in 1966 and the team had to finish the attraction without him. According to John Hench, someone got the skeletons for a cheap price from the UCLA medical lab (don't worry, most of them were replaced and laid to rest later). Since they had so many skeletons, they just went a little crazy adding them everywhere to the ride. So the original story Walt wanted to tell about the attraction got a little lost in translation because guests saw the skeletons everywhere.

Pirates didn't work as planned, so Disney went another way.

And the list goes on and on. Fantasmic was supposed to be staged in the moat of Sleeping Beauty Castle. Cinderella Castle was supposed to have a glockenspiel glass-slipper ceremony of Prince Charming and Cinderella just below the clock (where curtains are hung in a small M-shaped inset today). Frontierland was supposed to have Granny's Farm from the live-action movie *So Dear to My Heart*, but it just turned into a miniature horse corral instead.

None of that worked as planned, so Disney went another way.

The thing is, we all make our plans. We sketch out our futures, the ideals we aspire to and dream of making a reality. But things don't always go as planned.

I wonder, though, if life's not meant to always go as planned. Maybe it's meant to go another way.

And it's funny how, given enough time, the "other way" starts to feel exactly like how it was always meant to be.

On the Mark Twain

It was there from the very beginning

the idea of a paddle wheeler gliding along the water

in the earliest concepts

in the smallest parks.

Walt dreamed of navigating past snags and sandbars

lazily floating the Rivers of America.

It's how he collected Arrow Development,

though he favored their car-building skills

over their boat ones.

It's how he collected Joe Fowler,

though they argued over his "ditch."

But mostly he collected memories with his wife

a 30th "Tempus Fugit" celebration

since time had indeed flown by too quickly

they climbed aboard the sparking new sternwheeler in the park of Walt's
dreams

a replica dressed like a wedding cake

that chugged along on its maiden voyage

around a quiet pool of water in a former orange grove

Walt and Lillian in tow.

That night Walt made for himself the memory of which he'd been
robbed

since two times he'd tried to float down the real rivers of America

and two times he missed the boat,

once by a strike

and again by a Great Depression.

I wonder if his resolve to have such a steamboat

giving endless rides on sparkling rivers

was a gift to us

that no one should feel the disappointment

of missing the boat like he once did

because it will just come around again.

And so the *Mark Twain*

holds the great hope

that what we truly long for

is just around the riverbend

if we wait for it

long enough.

From This Island

From this island

ducks make way for canoes

gliding through the water with those weighing their regrets

the Columbia follows behind

a gentle reminder that not so long ago we were voyagers

where now we've learned to settle.

From this island

railroad cars chug by one-by-one

carrying weary passengers and napping children

puffing fluffy white steam clouds

and memories of a man who loved his trains.

From this island

people wave at strangers

and explore lost treasure

and remember what it was like to be fearless in exploration.

From this island

I'm alone but not alone

an island myself in a sea of humans who are all seeking their own path

we nod to each other along the way

acknowledging that this is all circular

our lives

the trails

the river

our islands.

We are allowed to be lost here

because having an adventure starts with finding a new direction

choosing to go beyond the known

to places we've only dreamed of exploring.

From this island

possibility surrounds me in every direction

yet it's easier to watch than to journey

to wave instead of row.

But crossing the river to the island of others

is a greater adventure

and even though it poses the greatest risks

it's the only way to truly see

all of my island.

A Pirate's Life for Me

The scent of bromine and 1967 drifts out the folding doors

beckoning us into a twilight we didn't know we needed

a haven of calm

a bayou of peace

with fireflies that dance like the hope we hold so gingerly

then darkness resets us

and the drops reveal who we really are.

Do we hold on tight or throw our hands up

as we fall into a new realm

one that tells a story of what happens

when we hold onto what doesn't last

and cling to worthless pieces

of what we think will change our lives

but all it actually changes is us.

Those piles of gold we chase and plunder

they stay when we go

but the people we ride in the boat with

who weather the storms of life by our side

they are the adventure

they are worth the journey

and they are the only horizon that will ever be worth the chase.

20

THE SPLASH MOUNTAIN PROBLEM

I held on tight to her shaking frame and wondered if I was a horrible mother.

The intimidating echo of the Burrow's Lament wound its way between us, cementing my four-year-old daughter's terror and further digging the knife of mom guilt into my heart. It was her first ride on Splash Mountain since she'd finally grown tall enough to experience it, and I had looked forward to sharing with her a piece of my childhood, complete with a trip to the Laughing Place and a long slide into the Briar Patch.

But as I sat in the final row of our Disneyland Splash Mountain log, holding onto her tiny quivering frame, I didn't see any joy or excitement in her eyes. I saw only fear. And I wished I hadn't made her go, hadn't convinced her that it would be okay, because each tear that fell down her face told me I had been wrong.

Have you ever had regrets like this? Where you look back and wonder if the choice you made, which felt right at the time, maybe wasn't the right decision after all?

I often wonder that about Splash Mountain.

Recently I was discussing with some friends of mine the danger of creating content about the history of Splash Mountain and the movie that it was based on, *Song of the South*. It's always been controversial, even from the jump, and I knew that addressing it was a veritable minefield filled with fueled opinions on all sides.

But I am not one to shove history into the dark corners when it is uncomfortable. I believe we have a responsibility to have honest conversations, and sometimes difficult ones, acknowledging what happened in the past so we aren't doomed to repeat it. So let's talk a little bit about the mountain in the room.

When Disney's *Song of the South* was released in 1946, many people didn't realize it was set in the post-Civil War Reconstruction Era, when slavery had been abolished. It was based on a collection of stories compiled by Joel Chandler Harris in 1881 called *Uncle Remus*, taking folklore stories he'd heard in the South and placing them in a plantation setting. While this collection has its own set of controversial practices (including the eye dialect Harris created to emulate his interpretation of the Deep South African-American language of the time), something the work *did* do well was establish Uncle Remus as a freedman. There was no doubt that the story took place *after* the abolition of slavery.

This is not the case for *Song of the South*.

Though Disney added some lines about Uncle Remus being a sharecropper to allude to his freedom, the lack of clarity about the film's time period combined with the stereotypes and "happy plantation life" portrayed didn't sit well with many. As time went on and our collective awareness of racial stereotypes was honed, what had been socially accept-able in the 1940s was no longer tolerable. And so, over time, *Song of the South* was shoved to the back of the proverbial Disney drawer.

Which begs the question: If *Song of the South* was so controversial, why did they pull it back out to create Splash Mountain, a massive e-ticket attraction, in the 1980s?

Song of the South reentered collective consciousness in the 1980s when it was re-released in theaters twice in the same decade. Merchandise and character meet-&-greets ensued in the parks, and I still have a book from my childhood during that era featuring all the Br'er characters and their shenanigans.

Because of the success of the re-released film in the theaters, it made sense for Imagineering to create an attraction using that story. Tony Baxter and the team worked with the NAACP and tested the concept with several focus groups as they went forward, sensitivity-testing how it would be interpreted by the culture at large. At the time, many people in the African American community were thrilled with the idea of finally having a story in the parks that wasn't Euro-centric and that featured a folktale that came from African American culture. Because of this, Tony still says, "I will stand by this today; there is not a thing in the ride that was detrimental to anybody. Whatever the controversy is that's come up has more to do with what the film is. I think we're way overboard on that kind of sensitivity."

But the success of the film wasn't the only reason they decided to create Splash Mountain.

It was also designed to honor Marc Davis's work.

In the 1980s, an attraction called America Sings, which Marc Davis had so lovingly created for the defunct Carousel of Progress theater in Tomorrowland, was aging. Tony looked at the 115 unique animatronics Marc had invented (some designed after his previously canceled concept for an animated film based on *Chanticleer*) and wanted to find a way to both honor the attraction while also repurposing the animatronics to save money.

Enter: *Song of the South*.

It seemed a perfect fit, to take some of the characters who were created to sing American songs throughout history and put them in the bayou to sing some other kinds of tunes. And, as a bonus, Tony didn't have to completely disassemble yet another one of Marc's great concepts (like he had done previously with Western River Expedition in the Magic Kingdom when he proposed pulling the runaway mine cart ride out and making it its own ride, known to us now as Big Thunder Mountain Railroad). I honestly believe, from everything that I've read, that the logic of it was to salvage and save a beloved attraction any way they could. And they did, repurposing many of the animatronics for Splash Mountain.

And so for years, many of us grew up singing Zip-a-dee-doo-dah and laughing along in the Laughing Place, not thinking of it as anything more than a cute story. *Song of the South* as a film had not been released on home video and only had limited theatrical releases (and none past 1986), and the meaning behind the characters didn't seem anything more than Bre'r Bear and Bre'r Fox getting tricked by Bre'r Rabbit. It seemed to be just a fun, silly tale that ended with us all singing about what a wonderful day it was as we shook water off our limbs and exclaimed how wet our clothes had gotten from the splashes.

This was why there was such anger from all involved when Disney announced a retheme. Anger from those who believed something with such a negative racial history should be so prominently placed in the park. And anger from those who had never viewed it in that light and felt like a piece of their childhood was being ripped away.

It took me a while, to be honest, to work through my own feelings on the matter. I sat with the knowledge that Mary Blair's colors were referenced from the original film for the attraction, and erasing them felt like scrubbing her legacy from that corner of Disneyland. I thought about the brilliance of Marc Davis's comedic characters and wondered if they would, too, be lost. And I thought about the iconic songs that had defined my days at Disney as a kid, when I would ride Splash Mountain over and over again when the line was short, running from exit to entrance *ad nauseam* until I was thoroughly soaked through.

But I also thought about how our social awareness has changed. How we've done more listening to each other, not minimizing but rather amplifying the voices of people who are brave enough to speak up about their experience. And how many didn't see Splash Mountain as I did; that it meant something to them that wasn't cute, or funny. I also watched as people I know and love felt represented for the first time with the change to Tiana's Bayou Adventure, and my heart broke a little realizing what this new attraction meant to them.

I will miss the Splash Mountain of my youth probably for the rest of my life. But embracing change with open arms was not just what Walt wanted for his park, it's what was necessary to celebrate a new story being told, one that for many was long overdue.

I sometimes wonder if any of the Imagineers look back at that season of creating Splash Mountain in the 1980s with the same momma guilt I had sitting next to my crying child in the back of that log. I hated the feeling that I had messed up so profoundly, missing the undertone of unease, the possibility of problems, in the wake of my excitement for the experience.

But I offered her what I thought was best at the time, with the limited knowledge that I had of what it would mean to her. I wasn't a bad mom; I simply needed to gather what I learned from the experience, grow, and adapt to what she needed in the future.

When I realized she wasn't okay, I changed course.

When Disney believed Splash Mountain was no longer okay, they changed course, too.

We have the capacity to love something dearly, while also accepting that it means something else to others than it means to us. Both can be true.

And the new songs we learn to sing from water-speckled seats, the ones that have the capacity to bring joy and healing to others, might just become beloved, too, over time.

Because, if we let them, blue skies and sunshine can also make for a wonderful day.

On The Skyliner

Flying over the chaos below

my mind is free to roam

beyond details and plans and schedules

to a moment of peace I didn't know I needed.

The wind ruffles my clothes and kisses my cheeks

and the silence is more golden than any sunset I could ask for

because life can feel like a nonstop cacophony

of failures and must-dos

but up here

there is only rest.

Rest for my feet

rest for my soul

rest for my mind.

This little cab is my respite

reminding me that being is just as important as doing

and how a simple tone can bring endless peace.

Rocking back and forth in the pause

I wonder if I could capture the feeling of being above

and carry it with me below

but before I can puzzle out how to do so

my journey resumes and I sigh

a mixture of relief and regret

balanced like I am on the cable above.

I fly into the station

at a speed I'm never ready for

but that's how life is

arriving before you're ready

and choosing to step out into the world, anyway.

21

MOVING AMERICA

What is the first country you visit in Epcot's world showcase?

My *Distory* podcast cohost Kirk is already rolling his eyes at this question because he knows what's coming (and maybe you do too if you've listened along with us). If so, I'm sorry for you (but not Kirk).

Most people would probably answer this question with either Mexico or Canada. But the actual answer according to Disney history might just surprise you.

Now, if you're a Disney history nerd like me, it's no secret that Epcot as we know it today was at one point going to be two separate parks.

The first park was going to be called Epcot Future World Theme Center. It would have a "Main Street of the future" so to speak leading to a Communications Corridor. Here, according to Disney's description, "The visitor will be exposed to a series of entertaining and instructive, information experiences and communication techniques." The areas planned for this park included energy, transportation, food, production, finance, education, information, healthcare, and oceanography. This park might sound an awful lot like the Future World we saw on EPCOT Center's opening day 1982, and there is a reason for that.

But before we go there, we have to talk about the other proposed park, known as World Showcase. This complex would have been located south of Magic Kingdom just across the Seven Seas Lagoon next to a Transportation and Ticket Center. It was a sort of permanent World Fair where countries could sponsor pieces of pie-wedge-shaped indoor spaces at varying costs, depending on the size of their investment.

In 1974, President of the Walt Disney Company Card Walker described this version of World Showcase as a place where "the nations of the world may participate on a permanent basis to demonstrate their culture and products." The idea of an international area in a Disney park came from Disneyland's never-built International Street which was planned to run parallel to Main Street U.S.A., but nixed before the park was even constructed in 1955. Walt's Progress City, the utopian futuristic community he'd dreamed of creating as part of the Florida project, also included a space for an international market. This was, of course, before the idea of people living in a Disney Experimental Prototype Community of Tomorrow was scrapped. To honor Walt's original vision, the name and idea of World Showcase was a play off of Walt's statement in the 1966 EPCOT film where he stated it would be a "showcase to the world."

In 1976, Imagineers had to scale back the EPCOT project because of the energy crisis and a lack of financial resources and sponsors. As the whole venture was at risk of being shelved, Marty Sklar and John Hench stepped in with an unusual idea to save the day. As Marty explained, "We originally started out to try to do two separate parks: one about countries around the world and the other about future ideas, and we couldn't get enough sponsorship to make that happen." He and John were supposed to meet with Card Walker and Don Tatum, and as Marty tells it, "We said [to each other], 'Unless we do something radical, we're not going to get this approved,'" so he and John Hench pushed the two models together to make one big park that could share infrastructure and therefore reduce costs. After a few hours in the model shop building a bridge between the two radically different parks, they presented it. Marty said they "did a wonderful job of being able to make these things match. And it worked. It's what is there today." Combining the two parks was a creative solution to finding a way forward, and what resulted was EPCOT Center as we know it today.

Well, kinda sorta.

You see, John Hench actually wanted the two parks to remain separate, and have a Monorail station in the middle of the two for easy accessibility to both parks. And the original plan after the two models were joined, was to have you enter through World Showcase (not Future World). The different countries of the world would then serve as a sort of international Main Street U.S.A. like the one abandoned at Disneyland over two decades before.

So, how did we get to the version that opened in 1982?

Well, in 1977 the Imagineers flipped the positions of Future World and World Showcase, and that was when the park began to resemble what we know it as today. Some of the locations of pavilions also moved around in Futureworld, like The Land pavilion relocating to the other side of the park, and a "Space" pavilion, becoming Horizons in the spot where they originally had placed The Land.

But that wasn't the only part of the park that had some drastic rearranging.

Over in the world showcase, only a handful of the 30 planned countries would actually be constructed, largely due to lack of sponsorship by countries or corporations (not for lack of trying). There were at least 18 different countries we almost got in World Showcase, including Russia, Israel, Switzerland, and Denmark, among others.

But one country was always planned, and that was America.

Yet it didn't quite look like what we have today.

It started as a large round building meant to house the grand American Adventure show, considered at the time to be one of the main highlights of Epcot. This building would be the connection point between Future World and World Showcase, and America was to play the role of "host" to all the other countries around the world. That's why it looked so different from the other countries ... it was a futuristic, circular building built up so that guests could walk under it on their way out to walk around the world. This is also, by the way, why this pavilion is still called The American Adventure versus simply the "America Pavilion."

Since you started in America, it's only natural that the first two choices you get are its neighboring countries—Mexico to the left and Canada to the right.

But that original big white circular building for the American Adventure is obviously *not* in Epcot today.

So why did this pavilion move?

Well, the party line was that it was a creative decision. That a good host "mingles" among their guests and doesn't separate itself from them. By shifting the pavilion across the water and changing its appearance to one that blends in aesthetically with the nations around the lagoon, America became a "good host" to all the nations.

But that wasn't exactly the whole truth.

The change wasn't so much a creative one as an operational one. Dick Nunis, known at Imagineering as "Hop-a-long capacity" (among other things), took a look at the plan for the American Adventure and balked. He saw what the creative minds didn't, a potential bottleneck of people all moving from Futureworld and then cramming into the American Adventure theater, wanting to see the spectacular new show first before moving around the world.

Dick was the one who suggested they move the entire pavilion to the center of the nations across the lagoon. Doing so would create what Walt Disney would call a "weenie", a term used when he would lure his dogs places by dangling hot dogs (or "weenies") in front of them.

The Disney parks are littered with "weenies," by the way, the visual hooks that pull you towards places. Just think of seeing the carrousel spinning through the arch of Sleeping Beauty Castle in Disneyland, or the Tree of Life beckoning you forward in Animal Kingdom. All are ways of pulling guests through the story, deeper into the parks.

Dick Nunis argued that by putting the American Adventure across the water, people would have the chance to wander the countries and take some photos, lingering along the way and dispersing the crowds. This would ensure the theater didn't get overrun by guests and help effectively manage capacity. Of course, this necessitated a redesign of the pavilion itself to not only make it visually intriguing from across the water but also make it fit in with the impeccably designed countries that surrounded it. It was no longer a gate from Future World, it was a country itself, a destination you looked forward to journeying towards.

It needed to change.

I don't think any of us would look at the American Adventure pavilion now and say, "Gee, I wish that was a big, white, circular building instead." No, the design of the colonial architecture is perfect to represent America's heritage as much as any country in World Showcase. And though it is still technically the "host nation," it *does* mingle so well in its new outfit that the theme of global unity is represented in a meaningful way, with America not lording over or dominating the other countries.

The change was good, and not just for operational purposes.

But change is hard.

I sometimes think about whoever designed that circular building, and how they wanted it to integrate with Future World. They put thought and effort into making it into a unique space to host a theater and still allow guests to flow through in the space beneath, creating a type of building not seen previously in a Disney park. Perhaps they were excited to see it come to life, expectant about how it would be.

And then it wasn't.

Plans change all the time at Imagineering, so, to be honest, I'm guessing they accepted that what would be would be.

But I still think about it.

Sometimes we live in the Future Worlds we've created for ourselves in our minds. When we think something we've planned, a relationship we have, or a project we're working on will go another way. We build our lives around what will be, trusting that it will be so.

And then it isn't.

Someone moves our American Adventure building, possibly without our input or permission, and we're lost standing on the other side of the lagoon, wondering what happened. How the thing we thought we *knew* was a given suddenly wasn't, anymore.

And then we start to question ourselves. Was it a flaw in our design? How did we not see this coming? What could we have done to prevent the heartbreak of watching all we'd hoped for disappear as if it never existed?

But here's the thing; The American Adventure was always meant to be across the lagoon. You can rail against it, lament it, question it, or argue its placement, but the reality is, it's there because it's meant to be.

And accepting *that* is what gives you peace.

That doesn't mean you can't choose to walk around the world and visit the new Colonial buildings. Maybe you even need to be a little bit sad at times that it's so many steps away, or that it doesn't look like how you thought it would be.

But standing in a beautiful pavilion while longing for another one only does *you* a disservice. In doing so, you miss *what is* while you mourn *what was*. It keeps you stuck, unable to explore new places because you can't let go of what you thought you'd have. Of who you thought you'd be.

The American Adventure changed. It wasn't what was planned.

But it's still good.

Yeah. Still good.

In fact, still important, despite its change. Knowing all of this, I feel like we can finally put to rest the age-old question of "Which country do you start in when it comes to the World Showcase" behind us. Despite our personal preferences of which direction we walk around the world, the true answer is, and always has been, clear: we all start, and end, in America.

Even if it's not where we thought it would be.

In Town Square

Disneyland's Town Square's purpose has changed throughout the years.

The center of the square was meant to be a "bandstand" for concerts to
be held

a gathering place for the community of Main Street U.S.A.

The gazebo was planned for that reason

but then relocated

when Ruth Shellhorn talked sightlines and views of castles with Walt.

The flagpole moved in, complete with a repurposed story of its own

and the words of opening day found a home at its base

but music was still played despite the gazebo's absence

albeit at a lower elevation

and trees and fences grew over the decades.

An evergreen joined the fray

when the park's main Christmas tree moved in

sometimes snuggling with the flagpole

but it needed its space

so more often it settled near City Hall

or replaced the drinking fountain that used to have a front-row seat

for horse-drawn trolleys and sparkling castles.

The square retained its shape but changed its clothes, its purpose

once a place of concerts

now a line for photos

once a drinking fountain

now a symbol for the latest celebration.

If someone time-traveled from 1955 and saw Town Square today

they might say

it looks the same

or

it looks different

and both would be equally true.

Each year we add shifts and changes us, too.

We build new fences to protect ourselves from careless people we shift our trees to make space to breathe

we realize fountains are ill-placed

we redecorate, renovate, remove.

But every shape we take is still us

just a new version of who we are

with the heart of the old

and our memories holding us up

like bricks under our feet

some a little wobbly or broken

we have no choice but to walk on them, anyway,

to make forward progress

letting each one support our steps.

And as we go on,

we raise our eyes to look around us

we realize

we are just like the square

same as we always were

yet different than who we used to be

Both.

Keep Moving
Forward

Pacing Mickey Mouse Park

Everyone probably thought Walt was crazy

pacing back and forth in an empty field next to Riverside Drive

across from Disney Studio

mumbling to himself and debating here or there for this ride and that

Roy didn't bother with his brother's bizarre little park idea

so sure it was just a fleeting notion

despite Walt's time in the field

but Walt kept going, day after day

consulting and studying and dreaming and mentally placing

covered bridges and mill ponds

fairgrounds and carnivals

gravity-flow canal boats

and a stagecoach traveling by Granny's farm

there had to be room for a steamboat to chug alongside Bird Island

a sanctuary for feathered friends

with skull rock

and a lighthouse for safety

of course, there would be a modest castle

and old town and new

embracing the past while welcoming the future

and a carrousel (with two Rs)

where all can ride

dads alongside daughters

on all jumping horses.

Some told him his dream was bigger than the space would hold

Walt didn't like being told what to do

but eventually relented

he didn't give up on his park, though

he just moved his pacing

to a different field

an orchard in Anaheim

and there he planted a dream called Disneyland.

22

THE DALMATIAN DISASTER

I once saw an interview that both broke my heart and inspired me all at the same time.

In 1984, Ken Anderson did an interview for the Disney Channel as part of a series called the Disney Family Album, reflecting back on his time at Disney. He had a prolific career with Disney, from an art director designing Snow White's cottage in the 1930s to developing Fantasyland for Disneyland. Walt Disney called Ken his, "Jack of All Trades," and he truly was a Renaissance man, able to do almost anything he was tasked to and do it well. And he did.

Well, except that one time he didn't, and Walt was horribly disappointed.

You see, in the late 1950s, Ken saw a problem that had plagued animators for decades and decided to do something about it. In the animation process, the animator's sketches were painstakingly traced onto clear sheets of celluloid (called "cels") by the women in the Ink and Paint department. With every hand tracing, though, the sketches strayed further from their intended original, fundamentally altering the way the drawings felt. As Ken put it, "Drawing has life because it's drawn out of your mind. When someone traces it, it becomes dead." Marc Davis also lamented this unfortunate part of the production process and said many times that his characters lost their charm and charisma when translated onto cels.

So one day, Ken (and Ub Iwerks - another legendary Disney animator) decided to do something about it.

The Xerox process was new technology at the time, but the idea of being able to directly copy animator's lines onto cels was revolutionary in his mind. No longer would any nuance or gesture be lost in translation; instead, the expression of the animator and their artistry would be on full display, unadulterated.

It was brilliant.

But since the technology was new, they decided to test it first for the Maleficent dragon in *Sleeping Beauty*. Though the scenes still went to the ink and paint department for finishing, the Xerox process experiment was seen as successful as it saved a tremendous amount of time. They found this technique also helpful for quickly replicating crowds of people in the film rather than hand-drawing hundreds of them.

Sure, it was a little rough around the edges, but it worked. It made everything faster, more cost-efficient, and maintained the integrity of the original animator's lines.

What more could you want?

Ken was elated. As they moved forward with the development of a new picture based on Dodie Smith's 1957 novel *The One Hundred and One Dalmatians*, he knew just what to do: finally make a Disney movie true to the animator's vision. Using these new techniques, they could accomplish that goal at a fraction of the cost of the disastrously expensive $6 million *Sleeping Beauty*, the most costly picture that they had made up until that point. The film had, unfortunately, fallen quite short of their box office expectations, and nobody wanted to repeat that failure.

The answer to all their problems was obvious to Ken: make the whole picture using Xerox to copy animators' sketches directly onto cels. Not only would it save time and money, but it would finally give the animators what they'd always longed for. That their work would be seen, fully, unadulterated by inkers or clean-up artists choosing which line to keep and which to toss.

And if you see *101 Dalmatians*, there's no doubt that the "rough" Xerox process is on full display. While one could argue it adds to the charm of the film, a unique artistic style, that was a full departure from every other Disney animated feature up until this point. Walt Disney had spent decades and millions of dollars perfecting the animation process to make it feel real, to make it believable, and to hide any hint that it was hand drawn or painted. Walt wanted to suspend reality and create a fully believable world that people wouldn't think of as just a bunch of "drawings."

I think some of this came from Walt's desire to be accepted in the film community. Many people dismissed his studio early in his career as not a serious contender for art and film because they only made cartoons. It was one of the reasons he wanted to make a full-length animated feature, in many regards just to prove that he could, and make the characters so heartfelt and believable that they would move people the same as any live-action could.

Eventually, Walt did get into the live-action film business, wanting to feel on an even playing field with his competitors (likely aided by the fact his post-war profits were also stuck in Europe). Walt saw live-action as a new challenge, a new frontier.

But animation was still where he'd gotten his start, and though he got too distracted by the building of Disneyland to pay as much attention to it, he still wanted his films to look a certain way, to be artfully produced. *Sleeping Beauty*, for what it lacked in story, was intended to be a masterpiece. As Walt said of the animated feature, "What we want out of this is a moving illustration. I don't care how long it takes."

And *Sleeping Beauty* was that, at least. A visual feast for the eyes, highly detailed and stunning in its perfection and precision. Though it failed to tug at the heartstrings the way many other Disney features had in the past (and lost the studio $900,000 after its initial release) it was every inch the artistic masterpiece Walt had hoped for, calling it the most beautiful film he'd ever made.

And directly following the *Sleeping Beauty* work of art?

Well, that's when we got the *101 Dalmatians* mess. Or, at least that's how Walt saw it.

Ken thought he had made a revolutionary discovery in using Xerox technology. They were progressing toward making Disney movies cheaper and more efficient to produce, while simultaneously allowing the animators something they'd always wished for, that their art would make it to the big screen unadulterated by another's touch.

It was the perfect solution.

But Walt didn't think so.

You could see all the pencil lines that Walt had spent years trying to erase. The style was chaotic and abstract, not precise and pretty.

He told Ken, "No more of that *101 Dalmatian* stuff" and publicly stated that Ken would no longer be an art director on his films because of what he saw as a massive failure.

Walt didn't talk to Ken for a solid year after that.

When you watch interviews with Ken Anderson, you can see the depths of the pain of that era in his eyes. That he let down someone whom he'd wanted to impress. Someone he wanted to make proud with his innovation, and instead he'd ruined everything.

It didn't matter that people loved the movie, or that it became a classic in the end. None of that mattered because Ken had failed Walt.

The year after the animator's messy lines were shown to the world, Ken had a stroke. And then another.

1962 found him paralyzed, unable to control his body the way he used to. He couldn't pick up a spoon to feed himself let alone a pencil to sketch. For a time, Ken even lost his sight.

Recovery was slow. While his sight returned and small gains in healing were made, it was excruciatingly snail-paced and frustrating. To keep his hopes up, his wife Polly took him on outings to a local park named Descanso Gardens, one they'd always frequented near where they lived.

And it was there he found the trees.

Above his head, they gnarled and spiraled, branches reaching toward the endless sky. Some grew at awkward angles or leaned this way or that. They weren't perfect, but they continued to grow, year after year. Ken later said, "If the oak trees could contort themselves into lovely shapes, if they could endure, if they were so strong to hold themselves in impossible angles" then maybe he could, too.

The trees inspired him to take three shaky, unsure steps. Then he added a few more. And over time, he regained his ability to walk, to move, to thrive.

Sometimes our mistakes can halt our forward progress. All we can see is our failure. How badly we messed up, that there is no way to come back from it. Maybe our failure causes us to lose people we love. The respect of people we cared about. Our sense of safety or self-confidence. Our health and well-being. Maybe we lose our tenacity, our determination to keep putting one foot in front of the other, too afraid we'll make another misstep.

We become Ken in his post-Dalmatian era, immobilized by our failure, staring up at the trees.

I imagine Ken could have given up easily then. Called it a day, said he'd already accomplished what he needed to, and it was okay to give up and let the earth reclaim him. But he didn't. He looked around and found that something else had been broken, stressed, and challenged, and it persevered. It endured year after year, and so he could too.

Ken called that moment his "redirection of life."

Your failure, that mistake you made, is not the end of you.

It's a redirection of your life.

It's a chance to try again, to take some shaky first steps in a new direction, to regain what was lost and push beyond it. It's a chance to become a new person with scars that tell a better story than any tattoo ever could.

And, eventually, you get to be the trees for someone else, proof that you endured.

Survived.

Didn't give up, even when all felt lost.

The last time Ken saw Walt before he passed, Ken said, "Gee, it's sure good to see you again, Walt." Walt was quiet for a moment, then responded, "It's sure good to be back, Ken." Ken said he didn't know how he knew it, but that was the moment he knew Walt had forgiven him for h is *101 Dalmatians* failure.

Maybe Walt forgave him. Maybe he let bygones be bygones after years had passed and he was at death's door.

Or maybe Ken had finally forgiven himself.

Because that's what gives you permission to put that self-berating story you've been reading for much too long back on the shelf; choosing to forgive yourself and let it go.

Too often we are still standing in our old failure long past the time when everyone else has forgotten it ever occurred. We feel like that's what we deserve, to be reminded of how we let someone down or made the wrong choice. We stay there, determined we aren't worthy of standing anywhere else. We become caged in by our choices, a prison we've built of our own pain, the bars made of memories and mistakes.

But the key to your release isn't dangling in the mouth of some mangy prison dog just out of reach; it's in your own hand.

You just have to decide that you deserve better than living out the rest of your days trapped behind the bars of your regret and shame.

Ken eventually recovered from his paralysis, moving on to create many beloved classics like *Robin Hood*, *The Aristocats*, *The Jungle Book*, and *Pete's Dragon*, among many others. Despite Walt's words, Ken did become an art director once again. And when it came time to renovate Fantasyland in Disneyland in the 1980s, he was asked to contribute his expertise, consulting on the creative direction for how to make Walt's favorite land in his beloved park anew. His artistic eye was trusted in a way I'm sure he thought it never would be again after Walt's disdain of his Dalmatians.

Ken's redirection made him stronger. He allowed himself to be transformed by his failure, and over time reclaimed his self-confidence, his self-worth.

You can reclaim yours, too.

You just have to look at that key, waiting for you in your hand, and decide to use it.

(And you *do* deserve its freedom. I promise.)

Twilight Thoughts

The chug chug chug of the C.K. Holliday reminds us

that life used to move a little slower

when sitting on the front porch

and watching the sunset

were nightly affairs

and we needed less

or, at least, weren't convinced we needed more.

I breathe in the scent of pine and desert

and wish I could see Walt and Lillian stroll down the sidewalks of Rainbow Ridge once more

or listen to the sounds of a swing band warming up in Plaza Gardens

ready to create the music that woos young hearts to fall in love.

As golden light surrenders to the purple blanket of twilight

we are reminded that our time here is fleeting

like those who built this place

and that what we do

who we love

how we live matters

because someday someone will walk where we walk

and see a sunset like this one

and question if how they spent their day was worthy of such a brilliant
end.

And I wonder

what they will think of

what they will remember of our world

when they do.

23

NO TIME FOR REST

Walt worked like he was running out of time.

Well, he was, in a sense. But he had no way of knowing that. Except for a fortune teller he visited once who told him that he would die prematurely.

Since Walt passed on at age 66, one wonders how much he would have done if he had kept going. What stories would we have? What attractions would have been dreamed up? What parks would have been constructed?

All unanswerable questions, to be sure, but a bigger one I often ask myself is what would it look like if Walt had rested more?

Walt hated being idle. Holidays and weekends annoyed him because he wanted to get back to work. Being away from the studio meant lots of communication back and forth, always a driving need to get back to his projects to see them through to completion. But there was not much time spent resting and celebrating before it was on to the next. That was just Walt.

Walt was also a bit of an insomniac. Some of his best ideas came to him in the middle of the night (something I can relate to myself). Perhaps his sense of impending demise drove his workaholism, feeling the pressure of doing all he could with the time he had left. He hated birthdays and getting older, perhaps because it reminded him of the clock running out.

Walt's nurse, Hazel George, gave him physical therapy every day for his old polo injury and witnessed this anxiety firsthand. It's what led her and Walt's secretary Dolores Voght to find a few pictures of themselves in their early 20s and sign their maiden names on them, giving them to Walt one year as a birthday present. They wanted to remind him that he wasn't growing old alone; that they, too, were not as young as they had once been, but that life was not over yet. Walt accepted the photos tearfully and hung them on the wall of his office.

I've felt like Walt.

Like I have so much I want to share with the world and such limited time to do so. It's driven me to stay up late, work endless hours, and put pressure on myself to keep producing nonstop.

Sometimes I wonder if Walt, like me, only felt like he was valuable as long as he was producing something. Like rest wasn't an option. Rest was for other people, and rest could only be earned after a sufficient amount of work had been done.

But rest isn't a commodity. It's a necessity. A lesson that Walt learned firsthand.

In 1931, Walt had a nervous breakdown. It was a culmination of many life events that caused his mental collapse, beginning with his bankruptcy of Laugh-O-Grams studio in 1923. That was followed by the stress of professional and personal betrayal when he lost Oswald the Lucky Rabbit and most of his animators to Universal via the villainous Charles Mintz in 1928. He bounced back with the debut of his new character Mickey Mouse the same year, but after his wife Lillian had a miscarriage and he lost his key animator Ub Iwerks to his distributor Pat Powers, he snapped. Walt was short with employees and had a hard time following conversations. He couldn't concentrate, and would sometimes randomly burst into tears as the stress got to be too much for him.

They say that if you ignore your body and don't rest, eventually your body will force you to do so, and that is exactly what happened to Walt. His doctor ordered him to take a complete rest in 1931, so he and Lillian set off down the Mississippi before heading to Washington, Cuba, and the Panama Canal. Roy took care of the studio in his absence, and when Walt returned, he began to innovate and expand, creating *Silly Symphonies* with color for the first time and a new depth of dimension with the invention of the multi-plane camera.

Rest was a reset for Walt, at a time when he could have easily said "I can't afford to rest." But he couldn't afford *not* to.

We often minimize our limitations and lean into the excitement of boundless possibility. I think when we are young we embrace this more fully, believing ourselves invincible, like nothing we do could ever harm us. My son lamented the other day that I am always telling him to be careful and that I am far too cautious. I simply replied that I used to take more risks before I knew more; my experiences and wisdom have taught me to be cautious over time (he still doesn't think I know what I'm talking about but he's a teenager and I know he will get it–eventually–when he's older, just like I did with my own mom).

As we age, we start to notice that we have more limits than we realized. That rest is no longer optional, and that our body will force us into it if we don't choose it first. And so we get to embrace our physical limitations instead of warring against them.

The place I find this to be the greatest struggle for me personally is in the Disney parks. I am an attraction-oriented park-goer, wanting to be immersed in story after story without end. My husband, on the other hand, is a "food and shopping" enthusiast, wanting to slow down and take it all in. I feel anxious at a long meal because of the rides I'm missing out on; he leisurely enjoys every bite and sees our conversations over plates of delicious food as the most memorable part of the trip. Both are valid ways of enjoying a day at Disney, but his is much more relaxing than mine.

Recently, I've decided to slow down more in the parks and simply take it all in. I no longer plan trips with wall-to-wall rides, but instead find space for enjoying the pauses, the moments where I can just be instead of endlessly accomplishing. I leave space for spontaneity, for discovering something new, and for doing nothing at all.

Walt Disney didn't lose momentum when he took a vacation with Lillian to rest his mind. Instead, he allowed his tired being to cease its striving and just be. He in turn came back refreshed and overflowing with new ideas, as is usually the case when we choose to trust that everything will be okay in our absence.

There will always be endless tasks to accomplish, bills to pay, and work to be done until our time is up. But we are more than the sum of our tasks. We are valuable because we exist, not because of what we've crossed off our to-do list or the accolades we receive from others.

Rest doesn't equal weakness, lack, or laziness; it's the peaceful pause that moves you forward into who you could never be without it.

Yale's Fireflies

The fireflies are dancing again

a simple thing but it lightens my heart

because it shows that someone cared for them

these little forgotten lights

still for so long in the dark.

I thought no one noticed

but someone did

someone revived Yale Gracey's invention

though his light went out long ago

they brought it back

instantly brightening the bayou

and illuminating the nostalgia of Pirates past.

The little fireflies are now visible

as we all should be

and it gives me hope that all who have been stilled

who have forgotten how to dance

will one day waltz in the moonlight once more

surrounded by others

who found their way in the dark

by making their own light.

24

ELIMINATING CONTRADICTIONS

It is one of the cardinal rules of Imagineering in the Disney parks, and when it's broken, it's jarring.

Eliminating contradictions, that is; making a cohesive visual environment is a main design principle that is the key to Disney's immersive parks. It's what keeps guests in the story. Anything that pulls them out has to go, be hidden or changed until what remains is believable. Visual contradictions, errant sounds, or unfinished interiors that give away the "how" behind the attraction are all counter to this rule.

Take, for example, how the inside of the Matterhorn was left rather unfinished when it opened in 1959. Long before the abominable snowman and the icy caves (those were added in 1978), the interior of Walt Disney's mountain was a giant mess of spaghetti-like roller coaster tracks. The exterior of the mountain was believable as an alpine bobsled, but crossing through the mountain was another story. You not only saw the mess that was an unfinished interior via the coaster, but those seeing Disneyland from the skyway gondolas also got an eyeful of ride tracks and steel beams as they drifted their way through the holes in the center of the mountain (when asked by a child why the holes were there, Walt once quipped, because it was "a Swiss mountain.")

Later, when designing Big Thunder Mountain, Tony Baxter and his team would work hard to design a dramatic landscape that appeared like the mountain had been there all along, and that the runaway train you boarded really was simply winding around its mines and buttes. All of the details designed to place you in the story, from authentic mining equipment from the 1800s to real mine tailings in the queue trucked in from the Tropico Mine of Rosamond, California (which, by the way, is also where *The Apple Dumpling Gang* was partially filmed once upon a time. The purple rocks are the more valuable ones, purchased for $120 a ton while the brown-colored tailings were closer to $80. But I digress).

We see this everywhere in the Disney parks. Meticulous details that pull us into the story and out of our own, truly getting to live in a world of Yesterday, Tomorrow, and Fantasy. It's what arguably sets Disney apart from its competitors, the incredible attention to research and development to make each attraction its own individual world. We've come to expect it, not even realizing in most cases just how much work has gone into eliminating contradictions to keep us in the story.

That is, until they forget to eliminate one.

When they first installed Avengers Campus next to the exquisitely themed Radiator Springs in Disney California Adventure, I was appalled to see that they completed the project without a visual divider between Mater's Junkyard Jamboree and the W.E.B. Workshop. The giant red building bearing the Spiderman emblem was clearly *not* designed to be in the dusty Southwest along Route 66, and yet it glares back at us defiantly as we swing around in our anthropomorphic tractors. There was a backstory created that explained away the land's proximity to the Stark Industries complex, but it's impossible to draw a connection to how the junkyard was Stark's scrapyard as you're watching tractors whip around with what feels like a ridiculously incongruent backdrop. The landscaping team has planted a few trees that I think eventually will grow to cover this incongruity, but until then, the visual contradiction between the two stories is one that we have to simply suspend disbelief or ignore altogether.

There is another, much smaller oversight in the queue for the Jungle Cruise in Walt Disney World. It's been there for years, and I suspect it will be there for many more to come, but it bothers me simply because it feels lazy to have overlooked it.

The Jungle Cruise is set story-wise in a British Colonial outpost in 1938. All of the props in the queue support this storyline, as does the Jungle Radio network you hear with Skipper Missy making announcements here and there (RIP Albert AWOL, Voice of the Jungle). Even the skipper crews (kind of like Hogwarts houses) tell the story of the timeline, with vintage photographs, props, and clothing.

However, when you get to the load area, there's a prop that is very specifically *not* from the 1930s or earlier. It's what appears to be an antique red metal gas can, which admittedly does look like it could have been used in a jungle outpost in the middle of nowhere. There are just a few problems: it's not a gas can, it's a jerrycan from France, likely used to carry wine as indicated by the French word for wine "VIN" emblazoned on the side. The can was also likely originally green and simply painted red by Imagineering. To be fair, both of these could easily be forgiven as most guests would not notice. But the worst contradiction of all to the story being told is the imprinted date at the bottom that says 1956.

Now, I know this is a little detail that many people won't recognize or care about. And that's fair. But with all the effort poured into the storytelling in this queue and eliminated contradictions, I can't understand why Imagineering has never thought to cover the date, replace the prop, or even just *turn it around* so the date isn't visible. Unless the "gas can" had somehow time-traveled from the land of sock hops and poodle skirts, there's no reason for it to be in a jungle in the 1930s. And it pulls me out of the story, every time.

But it also reminds me of our contradictions, ones we keep around in our own lives even though they don't make sense.

Sometimes this can take the shape of a job that isn't quite a perfect fit, but it does what we need it to do. We have a paycheck. We like our coworkers or are good at what we do, but something still feels unsettled in our souls, like we know it's not where we are supposed to be, but we stay, anyway, because it's easier. Why fix something that isn't broken, we reason.

All the while the part of ourselves that needs more, that craves adventure and purpose and that spark of knowing *you are doing what you were born to do*; that part becomes a contradiction that lives with us daily. Poking us in the ribs at the end of the day when we clock out and feel dissatisfied. Nudging us in our minds when we hang up the phone or check another box or sit in another endless meeting about something we couldn't care less about.

We become walking contradictions, knowing that something isn't how it should be, but still, we let the fear of chasing our dream hold us back from the story we were meant to live.

There are other contradictions that we fail to eliminate that go deeper. Like how we know that a particular person isn't good for us, but we keep them in our lives anyway, afraid to let them go. Terrified of what life would look like without them because they've become a comfortable contradiction. They may even steal our peace on a daily basis or treat us as if we are disposable, and yet we don't know how to eliminate them from our lives, so desperate we are to continue writing them into our story.

Or perhaps our contradictions are the ones we create within ourselves. The thoughts in our head that we aren't good enough, aren't capable or beautiful or worthy, even though we have a wealth of evidence to the contrary. We tell ourselves tales that aren't grounded in reality, letting our anxiety shadow the story, our hurt hold the pen. Somewhere along the way, we lose the plot, distracted by all the things that never belonged in our story, but we wrote them in any way, crossing out truths to make them fit.

Like any good Imagineer, it's our job to find our own contradictions and eliminate them, one by one.

I don't know if the gas can in the Jungle Cruise queue will ever change, or if the trees will eventually grow large enough to hide the incongruency of Avengers Campus from our rides on Mater's tractors. I don't have control over any of those contradictions. But I do get to choose what *I* do with the ones in my own life; the people, thoughts, and situations that simply don't fit the life I want to live.

And so do you.

Find your contradictions. Protect your story. And eliminate all the voices that tell you that you can't.

In the Push and Pull

When you step into Disneyland

there is a beautiful push and pull

that echoes our own journey.

Its a pattern of holding on and letting go

like how the trees provide shade and beauty

but some are also memorials

reminders that every life comes to an end

and what we do with ours matters.

There are pockets of lost ideas that almost were

and places that still hold fragments of what was

pieced together with new creativity

new vistas destined to become nostalgic for the next generation.

There is exquisite art created by a widowed baroness

and murals made by a mother

who couldn't protect her children from her husband

so she poured her heart into the innocence of painted ones.

Disney is the beautiful push-and-pull

of both

light and dark

humor and humanity

like us.

It's our story told in words

we can't quite find any other way

allowing us to be what we need to be

to simply rest

and be

in the middle of it all.

25

THINKING BEYOND THE BASEMENT

Years ago, someone once told me that I shouldn't bother trying to be a Disney creator because all of the successful ones were men. Or, if they were a woman creator, they were coupled with a man, and that was the only way anyone would take them seriously.

I balked at that idea. Surely there had to be strong women creators in the Disney community who were prosperous and making a positive impact on the world. But as I did a little digging, much to my dismay, I discovered that it was true.

All of the "big six" content creators (as they were known back then) were men. The historians, the same. All men.

I shrank back into the woodwork, seeing the writing on the wall and an uphill battle that I wasn't ready to climb as a mom with two small children. My days were busy sweeping up Cheerios and singing Disney songs to my babies, and so all of my dreams of writing and creating Disney content faded away with the hopelessness of reality.

The words that person said to me that day held weight. They sank my dream.

But I chose to carry them. I let them sink me.

I could have placed their opinions on the ground and walked forward anyway, but instead, I allowed them to hold me down, and hold me back.

Until I didn't.

I remember so clearly the Walt Disney World trip when I started to take my first tentative steps toward creating. My dear husband Eliot saw me taking a photo of something weird in the Jungle Cruise queue instead of our kids (though I took many of those as well). He then looked me straight in the eye, smiled, and said, "This is all leading to something, isn't it?"

I shrugged. I still carried those heavy words around at that time, believing that I could try but never be successful. But I had started to see a glimmer of hope, wrapped in a package of the Disney history I had studied for fun for years.

I started writing. Words that were close to my heart about how I saw the Disney parks, and how they carry meaning for us beyond the berm. I also started posting some of the things I'd learned along the way that I thought others may love knowing about as well. It wasn't (and isn't) an easy journey, and I've had many times when I've considered giving up. It took three more years of consistency, effort, and sometimes tears before I saw anything resembling progress.

Sometimes I think about my own journey alongside Walt Disney's. When he created new things that had never been done before, he called it "pioneering," and many of the early Imagineers used that same language to describe their work. They weren't wrong. Many films and projects imagined by the brilliant artists at Disney pushed boundaries and sometimes made up new ones altogether. Walt didn't stop when someone scoffed at his idea or told him it couldn't be done. He told them, "It's fun to do the impossible" before he walked away from their negativity and doubt. I think he truly believed that. And I think he was right.

When Walt set out to make the first full-length feature animation ever attempted in 1937, he and all his animators were dedicated to the project, even with the unknown looming above them. Many stayed late into the night and worked weekends at the studio not because they were required to, but because they believed in what they were doing. As Ken Anderson recalled, "We worked until midnight many nights. We worked on weekends. We didn't know that there was another picture in mind. That was the one picture. That was our one effort." I wonder then if any of the artists knew they were making history with their simple strokes of graphite, ink, and paint. The film wasn't a sure thing. I love how Ken put it when he said, "We knew how important it would be to us, to ourselves. But we never even considered the future beyond this picture. It was what we were going to do. We were going to finish this up and get back to the rest of our lives and live off of the love of what we'd done."

Before *Snow White* premiered, many people couldn't imagine a scenario where adults would want to sit through a longer version of the shorts that Disney was known for. Even the celebrities at opening night, who were required to attend for the publicity, looked down their noses at the picture before the screening, thinking it was a waste of time. And the trepidation even crept into Walt's own family. "I was afraid," said his wife Lillian. "Roy was too. But Walt wanted to do it."

Walt was a risk-taker. This was possibly something he inherited from his father Elias, who had bounced his family from city to city, forever chasing the next get-rich scheme. Walt seemed to embody that same sense of adventure, of trying something new and not being afraid to fail. That act of pioneering, of stepping out into the unknown where no one has ever dared venture, gave the world *Snow White* and countless animated films thereafter.

The Disney parks are filled with similar risks and adventures. As the Imagineers wove the magic of storytelling throughout Disneyland, so did they find their way around, over, and through the obstacles that threatened to hold them back.

Let's look at Pirates of the Caribbean, for example. In its earliest iterations, it was meant to be a simple wax museum called Rogue's Gallery. You would go down 70 feet into the basement of the Blue Bayou Mart and be faced with a series of vignettes (and yes, that's why the current restaurant is named similarly, which in turn got its name from the *Blue Bayou* short from *Make Mine Music* from 1946). Lights would then illuminate the wax pirates, and a track would play, telling you a tale. The pirates themselves were to be life-like but not animated, as this was before the days of audio-animatronics.

Pirates, like the Haunted Mansion, was a project put on the back burner when the 1964 New York World's Fair pulled away the WED (Imagineering) team to make four elaborate attractions for the world to see. There, they not only developed incredible new innovations based on declassified military and NASA technology, but the Imagineers also learned a thing or two about capacity; that is, how to get people through the attraction faster and more efficiently.

Pirates was to become a boat ride, allowing guests to quite literally flow through the attraction faster.

But that was not all they adopted from the Fair. The Imagineers figured out that you could have a façade "onstage" for guests to see, creating an immersive environment, but then put a show building behind it that was not visible to guests. And for the first time, they could grow beyond the basement that had restricted their creativity when it came to Pirates of the Caribbean.

The Imagineers started thinking outside the box, outside the limited space that was available in what is now the Ghostly Grotto portion of the ride. Putting the show building on the other side of the berm (and having us travel under the railroad tracks to get to it) opened up a world of possibilities. They started to create vast scenes and vistas, letting the pirates roam free in their imaginations to tell a bigger tale.

Sometimes I think we put ourselves in basements because we think that's all we have room for. Or maybe it's the place where someone has put us because their lack of vision limits their capacity to see what *could be* rather than what *is*. But maybe if we think outside the box, outside the basement, outside the *berm*, we create space for things in our lives we never thought were possible.

People who are stuck in their basements like to keep others in theirs. But you were meant for more than keeping your talents and dreams inside the box others hold out for you to hop in. You're meant to find adventure in the great wide somewhere, pioneering and letting possibilities lead you down new paths until you find the one that was meant for you.

If you're feeling stuck in your own Blue Bayou Mart basement, start looking for your own show building outside the boundary you've created in your mind. Search for a new way, a new perspective, and don't let what currently is limit you from what could be.

And, by the way, women absolutely can–and should–be Disney creators.

26

We Can't Go Back

Walt would be rolling in his grave.

If I had a dollar for every time I heard someone say that, I could finally afford all the orthodontic work my three kids seem to endlessly need.

Usually, this is said by someone lamenting a change in the Disney parks. The cost. The "lazy" Imagineering. The magic that, according to them, is completely gone.

But the question is, would Walt actually hate what the parks have become? Or is this what we assume he would feel, wanting an ally to stand beside us in our sense of injustice and hurt?

Putting aside the fact that Walt was, in reality, cremated and not able to turn anywhere even if zombies did exist, I often ponder this question of how he would feel about what Disneyland looks like today. Or what Epcot became. Or the changes Roy made to his Magic Kingdom plans.

Now, I'm not saying that Walt would be thrilled with everything as it is. Clearly, his hope to make the park affordable and give the public a "fair deal" seems to have shifted culturally within the company as I look at

$100 spirit jerseys and $17 balloons. Micheal Eisner was the lynchpin in the mid-1980s to the ever-rising ticket costs that we brace ourselves for every year, especially as inflation makes it harder for us to afford groceries, let alone a trip to the Most Magical Place on Earth.

In contrast, Walt Disney argued against raising the price of parking over 25 cents. He wanted to make The Plaza Inn a place of affordable luxury for the blue-collar worker.

He wanted to make ordinary people feel special.

So, okay. I can get on board with the frustration that the everyday worker now has a hard time being able to afford walking through the gates of Disneyland to be able to access the Plaza Inn. And that the breakfast there is a pricey character-dining affair.

But you know what? They could have changed that restaurant to a sit-down, upscale exclusive dining establishment like Walt's restaurant in Disneyland Paris. But they didn't. For lunch and dinner, you can still walk in and get a delicious, relatively affordable plate of fried chicken just like Walt used to do at the Chicken Plantation house all those years ago.

(Sidenote: Disney, if you're listening, the Walt's restaurant idea was not an actual suggestion, we really don't want the Plaza to change. Please and thank you).

Another lament I often hear is how everything is Intellectual Property (IP) based, instead of the Imagineers coming up with new park-original concepts. To this I say, what do you think Walt Disney did?

Pirates of the Caribbean was inspired by Disney's 1950 live-action adaptation of *Treasure Island*.

The Matterhorn was inspired by the film *Third Man on the Mountain*. In fact, Walt was on location in the alps when he sent a postcard back to WED Enterprises with a picture of the Matterhorn, with just the words "Build this!" scrawled on the backside.

The Haunted Mansion was a hodge podge of ideas from *The Adventures of Ichabod*, *Fantasia*, *Snow White*, and a dozen or so popular horror movies throughout history (including the *Loved One* from 1965, which I believe is why you hear the ghost host say "Take your *loved ones* by the hand" when you're waiting to board your doom buggies.)

Mine Train Through Nature's Wonderland was based on Disney's documentary film series called *True Life Adventures*, as was the Jungle Cruise (though it had an assist in inspiration from Harper Goff's favorites like *Mogambo* and *The African Queen*).

And let's not even get started with Fantasyland, in which every opening day ride was solidly themed on Disney IP (Dumbo the Flying Elephant, Peter Pan's Flight, Snow White and Her Adventures, Mad Tea Party... you get the gist).

My point is, Imagineering has been basing rides off of Disney IP since the very beginning of Disneyland. It's not a new concept. It's the company's legacy.

So if Disney wants to design rides based on this current generation of children's favorite movies, why are we getting so upset about it? Especially knowing those rides will become nostalgic for them, places they will look forward to taking their own kids someday because it becomes part of what Disney means to them.

I think we are bothered by it because we want to go back.

When we watch our own childhoods being erased, bulldozed, and painted over, *it hurts*. Especially for those of us old enough to watch the houses we grew up in and the streets we used to live on completely disappear. Or have the people we loved fade away one by one. To us, all of the construction walls feel like someone kicking over our favorite sandcastles while our cries of protest fall on deaf ears.

When everything else won't stop changing in our lives, Disney sometimes feels like the only constant.

Until it's not.

So we shake our fists at any change, watching what we loved for a lifetime be cut from our lives in permanent slices. It's a brutal reality we're never really prepared for.

Because, as it turns out, it's not Walt turning in his grave; it's *us*. Twisting in our discomfort for having to encounter yet more loss in a world that feels like it's handed us nothing but.

The truth is, when I look at places now that used to be something else, I feel sad, just like everyone else. I miss singing Zip-a-Dee-Doo-Dah at the end of Splash Mountain. I wish I could experience the magic of the Rainbow Caverns or enjoy a twilight sing-along at Big Thunder Ranch one last time. And I'll forever miss the witch coming after us with a boulder at the end of Snow White's Scary Adventures, including the way the doors used to swing open to a cheery "And they lived happily ever after!" that felt so ridiculously incongruent that I couldn't help but laugh.

But something I've learned during the years I've been on this earth is that we can't go back, and staring over our shoulder too long just makes us run into lampposts and other churro-wielding Disney fans. We can't change the past. We only get to decide what we do now, what direction we face. What steps we take. What we see when we look at places that aren't what they used to be.

We can spend our whole lives being bitter about a change we didn't like. A circumstance beyond our control. Or we can make the best of what we've been given, making our peace with what *is* rather than what *was*.

I don't know about you, but I don't want to keep turning in my proverbial grave wishing things were different. I want to be at peace, accepting with grace what I've been given, and looking forward to a great, big, beautiful tomorrow.

I find that when I stop looking over my shoulder and shift my view to what's ahead, my whole perspective changes. It doesn't mean that I don't love and care about what's behind me, I just don't let it keep me from seeing what *could be* rather than what *used to be*.

We may feel uncomfortable with change, and unsure of the new stories that Imagineering is telling. But maybe if we look for the heart and love that they are pouring into creating the next generation's memories, we may start to see a new legacy being created, right before our eyes.

We can't go back. But we can find joy in what's ahead if we choose to.

Because we *will* make new memories. More moments in new places with the people we love. And the places we rallied against will soon become filled with all the joy and laughter we thought were lost along the way.

And before you know it, you're singing new songs that fill the cracks the old ones left behind.

And it's the Happiest Place on Earth, once more.

Because you kept moving forward, just like Walt wanted.

Build This

The icy slopes of Matterhorn Mountain

once were going to be a bit more chilly

with real snow

real toboggans

real cold on hot summer days.

But they realized it would be impossible to manage

impossible to create in a place known for sun and warmth

so the idea shifted to an icy slope of a different kind

a majestic mountain

miniaturized

first open on the inside

with skyway onlookers flying by

then enclosed

as an abominable snowman made himself at home.

A star graced the top

and climbers rappelled down.

Tink took flight from its snowy outcroppings

and millions have laughed as they jerked to a stop

at the end of their bobsled run

reciting words they've heard again and again.

The Matterhorn is our own mountain

created for joy

a snowy adventure

that doesn't promise a smooth ride

or any real snow to speak of

but this first Disney coaster

this first Disney mountain

is what we need

to shake loose our expectations

the idea that life is without bumps or bruises

and instead embrace them.

This icy slide around and through the mountain we're facing

is all just part of the adventure that Walt knew we needed

when he wrote two simple words on a postcard:

"Build this."

As we look back at the mountain

created from an idea

it's like a challenge

a call to action for our own dreams that we thought were impossible

just because we haven't found a way to build our Matterhorn yet

doesn't mean we can't have snow in California

we just have find a new way forward

and let what wasn't meant to be

melt away in the sun.

27

(DON'T) STICK TO SHORTS

If it was unfamiliar, people rejected it.

That seemed to be a common theme in the story of Walt Disney's life.

When he wanted to share his very first *Silly Symphony* with the world, no one wanted to distribute the macabre *Skeleton Dance* because they thought it too grim for general audiences. But Walt Disney believed in the work, so he premiered it himself in the Carthay Circle Theater in Los Angeles and the Fox Theater in San Francisco in 1929. Eventually, the short was picked up by Columbia after being proven successful with theater-goers, but reviews were mixed about the lighthearted skeletons rising from their tombs.

Variety magazine in New York published a review stating that *The Skeleton Dance* was high in its laugh count, but also warned that the short "all takes place in a graveyard. Don't bring your children." *The Film Daily* had a more glowing review, stating, "Here is one of the most novel cartoon subjects ever shown on a screen ... it is a howl from start to finish."

Silly Symphonies were meant to be a second source of revenue stream alongside Mickey Mouse, since the illustrators were limited in what they could do with Mickey in a way that they were not with the *Silly Symphonies*. The musical-based shorts were a place of experimentation for Disney, a medium where they could invent new techniques and ways of storytelling and not risk Mickey's reputation along the way. When they first introduced color cartoons, it was with the 1932 Silly Symphony *Flowers and Trees*. As they developed dimensional technology with the new multi-plane camera, they experimented with it first in The Old Mill in 1937. Finding the parallax effect successful, it was then implemented in the first ever full-length feature animation *Snow White and the Seven Dwarfs*.

But *Snow White* was not a given success. Many called it "Disney's folly" because they believed no one would want to sit through a full-length "children's cartoon." Walt was even unsure of its reception, as there was some mixed feedback about the film in the preview process. During an early screening of the movie, some people got up and walked out of the film. He later learned that those people had somewhere to be that was unrelated to the movie, but Walt panicked. What if everyone did that on premiere night?

Even more frustrating was receiving anonymous feedback about the film in a pre-screening, when someone at the studio simply wrote: "Stick to shorts." That comment stuck with Walt for years, and often when someone disagreed with him or criticized a project, he would point at them and say, "You're the guy who said stick to shorts!"

When it came time for *Snow White*'s premiere, sentiment hadn't yet shifted in Walt's favor. People looked upon his project not as a new art medium, but as a silly project trying to turn something as simple as a cartoon into a full-length feature. Celebrities showed up, but many were there because of pressure from their publicists, and animators mingling in the lobby before the show heard many grumblings and complaints about their need to attend such a trivial event.

All that changed, however.

Moviegoers had never witnessed a cartoon that could make them cry, but there it was, with Grumpy shedding a tear over someone who opened up his heart and who now lay lifeless before him. Animator Bill Tytla was known to embody his characters, and he'd animated this one so convincingly that the audience wept alongside the seven dwarfs, moved by the depth of human emotion captured in ink and paint.

It was a triumph of a film, but no one thought it would be before seeing it.

Disneyland was the same way.

The critics were ruthless when it came to predicting Walt Disney's failure in building a theme park. Another folly, they suggested. His competitors told him that he needed to buy off-shelf rides like carnivals had in order to be successful. Critics lambasted his idea of having a non-revenue-producing castle in the center of the park, highlighting its pointlessness if it wasn't an actual attraction (the inside walk-through part wasn't added until 1957, so it truly was just for aesthetics when Disneyland opened in 1955). People criticized his focus on cleanliness and landscaping, claiming people didn't really care or notice those details. They told Walt Disney he didn't know what he was doing, that he would lose his shirt incorporating so many details that didn't produce revenue, and that he should leave the amusement park business to those who knew it best.

But Walt wasn't making an amusement park. He was building another world. A world where people could step out of their everyday lives and into a story. A theme park unlike any other in the world, created from inspiration from other places but transformed through the lens of a filmmaker and storyteller.

Imagine if he had let those words stop him. If he had thought, "Well, they have a point. Maybe this is a stupid idea" and just dropped the Disneyland project altogether? What if he had chosen to just "stick to shorts" and never produced any films beyond *Snow White*?

Creating something new often makes people uncomfortable. They want to put you in a box, *their box*, categorize you in a way that fits their worldview and settles your definition in their minds. That is where every one of those comments came from. They were opinions stated as fact. Opinions of people who had a narrow vision only for what existed, and not for what *could* exist.

Walt Disney had an innate ability to see what would resonate with people, and wasn't afraid to put himself in a project whole-heartedly when he believed it would produce something good. People didn't always understand his process, but when they vocalized their doubt, he set it aside and kept moving forward.

He didn't let the words of a few small people make him small, too.

Because that's all they are, those who talk us down from our dreams and ambitions. The ones that try to stuff us into too-small boxes when our dreams outgrow their limited perspective. The people who leave nasty comments on our social media and the family members who throw ice water on our enthusiasm, they are simply trapped people actively resenting your expanding boundaries.

Walt Disney could have given up. On *Silly Symphonies*. On *Snow White*. On Disneyland. But he could see beyond the pessimistic words of a few small souls to the hearts of a million others.

He didn't give permission for their criticism to halt his dream.

And neither should you.

Folly

Folly.

Lacking good sense.

That's what people said about Walt Disney.

A mouse no one recognized.

A full-length feature animation.

A theme park.

A castle just for aesthetics.

All of it, folly.

It looked like it, from the outside.

From those who saw only what had been

instead of what could be.

Walt saw more.

He took those voices and tuned them out

drawing-creating-building anyway.

Let them think it's folly.

let them scoff

let them criticize

let them wait for you to fail.

Let them.

Then go do it, anyway.

Let their folly be your fuel.

Ghostly Resolutions

Starting today, I will stop dancing with the ghosts of my past

the ones who didn't think me worthy enough to treat well

who saw right through me as if I didn't exist.

I will let them go

bury their memory six feet under

and celebrate the breath in my lungs

as I toast new adventures with the living.

Today I will listen for words of wisdom

instead of chasing my own thoughts.

I will hold space for those I love

and hold boundaries

for those who don't know how to love me well.

Today I will no longer be held back

by small words from smaller people

or let comparison steal my focus.

I will not let the wounds of my past turn my heart to stone.

Today I will find a way forward

knowing my scars strengthen my story

and healing is holy ground.

Today I will not be afraid to feel

will not go numb and withdraw when it's scary

and instead will lean into the wind

knowing that it will embed my roots deeper in the soil

and make me stronger in the end.

Today I will look in the mirror

and have compassion

for the reflection that looks back at me

knowing what its been through

and instead of being haunted

I will let my pain become a friend

as we surface together from the darkness

and dance our way into the light.

28

PREDICTING THE FUTURE

Tomorrowland is the land of a perpetual identity crisis.

While the "Land of Tomorrow," as it was going to be called, sounded futuristic and novel in the Atomic age in which it was invented, the speed at which it was assembled at Disneyland didn't take into account the problem of predicting the future. The Imagineers didn't foresee how they would have to reinvent the land again and again in the years to come as the future became the present and then the past, over and over.

The original plan for Tomorrowland was to make it the "Futuristic World of 1986" when Halley's Comet would make its appearance in the sky. Despite the fact that French astronomer Camille Flammarion associated the comet with the demise of the world as we know it (apparently "The cyanogen gas would impregnate the atmosphere and possibly snuff out all life on the planet"), it was an astronomical phenomenon that signaled the zenith of the Space Age and fascinated a generation. Since there was no roadmap to the future, the Disney Imagineers dreamed up their own kind of Tomorrow. As Ward Kimball put it, "Projection into the future could best be attained by animation, since it could not yet be photographed."

The Tomorrowland part of Disneyland was almost canceled altogether in January of 1955 since budget and time didn't seem to allow for the land to be created. CV Wood argued that it was impossible to complete given the short window they had left to create the vision for Tomorrowland, and Walt Disney reluctantly agreed. The Land of Tomorrow went on the shelf, earmarked for completion after the July 17, 1955 Disneyland opening date (which was locked in by their ABC *Dateline: Disneyland* television show premiere). It didn't take long though before Walt reversed his decision, saying, "We'll open the whole park. Do the best you can with Tomorrowland, and we'll fix it up after we open."

And so Tomorrowland was hastily thrown together in a flurry of aluminum and sponsored attractions in only six months. A V-2 rocket inspired by Werner Von Braun's designs went up in the center, a wooden structure covered in the sponsor Kaiser Aluminum's product from head to toe. It was known to make a series of loud bangs each morning and evening as it expanded and contracted from the heat of the day.

No one said creating the future was easy.

That certainly continued to be the case in the years to come. Tomorrowland was a motley assortment of futuristic–and odd–choices for predicting what would be, combined with sponsored attractions. A dairy bar, an art corner, the Monsanto Hall of Chemistry, and the Crane Plumbing Bathroom of the Future all found their way in and out of Tomorrowland, among many others. And from 1957 to 1967, the entrance to Tomorrowland held the crown jewel of them all: The Monsanto House of the Future.

It was a 1960s dream house of fridges for all your irradiated foods, video doorbells, sinks and counters that raised and lowered as needed, and cabinets that would wash your dishes for you with an ultrasonic dishwasher. It had a revolutionary microwave oven, touting its ability to bake a potato in just three minutes. All the walls, floors, and ceilings were made of plastic, and everything within the house was man-made. Organic anything was persona non-grata in this futuristic house meant to promote Monsanto's chemical innovations, and the wonders of plastics were on full display.

Whether or not this building ideology was beneficial to the humans living within the house (or the world outside it) wasn't a consideration at the time, as technological innovation was seen as progress, and progress was the future.

But the future eventually becomes the past, and the House of the Future soon became outdated, only a decade after it had been installed. With the addition of the newer and more engaging Adventure Thru Inner Space attraction (also sponsored by Monsanto), the House of the Future became the past. They brought in the wrecking ball and took down the plastic white house (taking a few more swings than they anticipated since it was so well-built). The concrete base stuck around, still (sort of) there today, just covered with some army-grade camouflage netting. Tomorrowland faced similar deconstruction in 1966, reopening as a much more well-defined and planned-out land in 1967.

Years passed, and, despite additions like Space Mountain and Star Tours, once again, Tomorrowland started to show its age. Plans were made in 1993 for a "Disneyland 2055" revamp including a Wall-E Synergy Initiative and the PeopleMover replaced with an attraction called the Rocket Bikes (think: Tron bikes traveling at high speeds on the People

Mover tracks). But none of these futuristic plans became reality, as they were scrapped when the Euro Disneyland project put financial strain on the company.

In 1998, Tomorrowland was reimagined yet again, borrowing the retro-steam-punk vibes of Disneyland Paris's Discoveryland (ostensibly to save money by not reinventing the wheel). This was merged with an "Agrifuture" concept, leaning on sustainable agriculture and edible landscaping to provide a "futuristic" footprint on the land, one that can still be seen today in grapevines, herbs, and fruit trees. About 80% of the plants in Tomorrowland today have edible elements, but guests are discouraged from snacking on them, not only for aesthetic purposes but also for safety as not *all* of them are 100% edible. If you've heard that all the plants are edible, well, that was just a story that people made up after hearing an interview from Tony Baxter in 1999. He was simply enthusiastic commenting on the transformation of Tomorrowland, saying, "We went from the cliche of dark images of the future to a veritable Garden of Eden, where every plant in Tomorrowland is edible."

The "new" Tomorrowland of the late 1990s no longer looks so new. It's due for a facelift, one that many of us have been waiting for with bated breath.

Because Tomorrowland has an identity crisis.

It wants to predict the unpredictable. Become something that will be. But all it seems to have been able to do is aggregate what the past believed the future to be, getting trapped in a wheel of space-age retrofusion again and again.

I think we all feel like Tomorrowland sometimes.

We want to create a new future but get stuck in our past.

The people who shaped us, good and bad, play on repeat every time we try to make something new out of our situation.

It can keep us in a box and limit our creativity, our ability to think bigger than what we already know. We start to think maybe this is just how it is, and shrug our shoulders at the aging Tomorrowland of our world, believing it's all the future that is possible, given our past.

But that wasn't Walt's vision for Tomorrowland.

The dedication for Tomorrowland, the words that shaped his vision for the land, said this:

A vista into a world of wondrous ideas, signifying man's achievements ... a step into the future, with predictions of constructive things to come.

Tomorrow offers new frontiers in science, adventure and ideals: the Atomic Age ... the challenge of outer space ... and the hope for a peaceful and unified world.

Tomorrowland wasn't meant to be just about tomorrow. It was always meant to be about ideas, adventure, and challenge. It's embracing the impossible and making it possible. It's building something new that's never been done before so that we can give the world something meaningful (and needed).

Tomorrowland was a dream, an experiment in thinking about what *could be* rather than only what *was*.

We're not always going to predict what will happen when we take a risk and build something new. But that doesn't mean it isn't worth creating.

The alternative is to just keep repeating the past, a *Groundhog Day* of our own making because we let the fear of innovating keep us rooted in yesterday's thinking.

Your past will always give you reasons why you shouldn't dream about your future. But the failures of your own Tomorrowlands to become what you'd hoped doesn't mean that the next version isn't worth striving for.

Even if it turns out you don't need the irradiated fridges and three-minute potatoes, they all serve a purpose in getting you where you need to go.

Your House of the Future is waiting, camouflaged in nothing but your own doubt.

Go find it.

You deserve a future that's not held back by the past.

A Closed Window

It made them uncomfortable

when Disney's animators

reached to open the window in their new office

and were scolded for doing so.

Air conditioning was novel then

keeping the studio temperature sustained

the humidity managed.

It was done to protect the celluloid

on which the heart of each film was painted

and to keep dust away from camera lenses

but it was unsettling

this enclosure

when they simply wanted fresh air like they had always had before.

They didn't understand the harm it could do to a delicate system

they simply wanted an open window

a light breeze

to hear birds chirping over the alien noises of whooshing air ducts.

They longed for what was.

They didn't like change.

Sometimes we find ourselves inside a studio

standing by the window and clawing at the frame,

trying to find a way back to what we once knew

what we were comfortable with

we don't see the harm that could come from opening a window to the past

and don't want to see the benefit of the air conditioning

when it feels like our window handles have all been removed.

But when we pause and let the coolness surround us

when we no longer have threats of dust and damage

we start to see

that what we want and what we need aren't always the same

and grow comfortable in the silence between what was and what is

letting the new air fill our lungs

and accepting our limitations

our loss

because soon we discover that

a closed window still welcomes the sun.

29

WAITING BY WALLS

A few months ago, I walked the elongated construction detour to Concourse E at Portland International Airport as I'd done so many times before, headed back to the Disney parks I know and love. As I passed the same window that had watched me walk past, time and time again, I paused.

It was dark.

For months, I had dragged my not-a-morning-person exhausted self down that long hallway knowing that at the end, I would be rewarded with a sunrise view of Mt. Hood perched above the line of planes waiting to fly over its peak. But this morning, the window was dark.

I couldn't see the white snow gleaming atop the mountain where I'd said vows to my husband almost 20 years ago. Couldn't see the pinks and reds and yellows of the rising sun. Couldn't see, well, anything at all.

The light had shifted. The view I'd grown to know so well was suddenly gone.

The feeling was akin to when you arrive at the Disney parks and race to your favorite ride, only to find it surrounded by a long, green construction wall. We get so used to something being there that we feel the ache of its absence acutely once it's gone.

It's that way with people we love, too.

We expect that some people will always be around. Their presence is just a constant, a given. Be it a parent, or spouse, or friend you've known so long you could easily finish each other's sandwiches; we tend to think of people as permanent attractions rather than temporary exhibits. This leaves us startled when construction walls halt our forward progress down the paths we know so well. When people grow, or change, or move, or leave. Suddenly we are bereft of that previous connection, shut out because we aren't part of the construction crew. We can't go where they've gone.

It's uncomfortable, standing on the other side of the wall from what we love. We don't know what they are doing in there. Are they changing what we've always known? Altering the attraction in some permanent way that will steal its nostalgia? It's simple joy?

The unknown is *maddening*. Imagineering could be doing anything behind those walls, and except for a few concept art posters tacked up on the temporary wood and plastered as "breaking news" on every Disney influencer's social media pages, we are left in the dark. We peer through cracks and try to catch odd angles where we can see something, *anything*, about what we can expect.

But in the end, we have to wait and see. We have no other choice.

We can't speed up other people's construction. As much as we want someone to be who we need them to be, sometimes they may take a long time to get there. Or perhaps, by the time their construction walls come down, they will have changed so much that we don't recognize them at all. We lose the connection, the memories still held in the same location, but the appearance altered in such a way that we never quite feel the same way about it again.

Maybe the changes were good. Needed for the ride. New tracks, or theming to draw in guests, or layers of paint to brighten it up after years of fading in the sun. Perhaps we can even admit to ourselves that the new version is an improvement, even while our hearts are heavy knowing everything we once knew has changed.

The hard truth is that people, like attractions, all change, eventually. Even the ones we think haven't ever changed, like Sleeping Beauty Castle.

Once upon a time, Disneyland's castle had ivy that crawled up its walls. The ivy started small in the 1950s and '60s, but by the time my tiny two-year-old self was photographed strapped into a maroon and metal stroller in the 1980s, the ivy had taken over most of the left and right sides of the castle. It wasn't until Disneyland's 50th anniversary that the invasive plant was finally removed, likely due to the arrival of projection mapping and additional pyrotechnics that required a clean surface on the front. Its removal, however, permanently altered the look of the castle for those who had grown used to seeing it adorned with rich greenery.

It was a change.

The castle has also been dressed in brighter colors than the pale pinks and blues that it wore on opening day. Various anniversaries have seen the addition of stained glass windows, gold accents, and banners changed time and time again. The trees have also grown and matured around Sleeping Beauty Castle, dwarfing it in the process. While its spires and turrets used to tower above the park, a visual landmark from any land, the 77-foot landmark now seems diminutive, pony-sized in a way I don't think the original Imagineers intended. Its forced perspective has been betrayed by the landscaping, and while the castle is charming, even the most stalwart Disneyland fan (myself included) has to admit it looks, well, quite *small*.

It's changed.

But so have we.

When I was that tiny two-year-old, or even later at age six, I remember walking over the drawbridge, hearing "When You Wish Upon a Star" and marveling at the castle. It was *spectacular*. There was nothing small about it. It was a real, massive fortress that housed princesses and dreams.

As I got older and taller, the castle gradually shrunk, year by year. But that doesn't mean I don't still stand in front of it, remembering that awe of my younger self and the dreams she used to have. The castle's reflection has been altered, but so has mine.

Greenery was what I knew, but it had to be removed to make room for something new. It was time.

And so, as I stand on the other side of the construction walls from people I used to know, separated from all the memories and the life I once had, I have a choice. I can stand and stare at the green wall, anxiously waiting for it to come down, wringing my hands about what I will find when it finally does. Worrying about what will be left of what I used to know.

Or I can choose to walk away.

Walking away feels *impossible*. Not when so much is at stake. But I can't hurry construction along by waiting and watching. Nor can I change what the attraction will become. So I have to let it go. Let it be what it will be.

I need to go ride another ride.

That doesn't mean I can't go back and check on the walls from time to time. See if the ride is open again. If it's ready for me to see it in its new iteration. But I can't stop enjoying the rest of the park simply because a favorite ride is closed for a season.

We have to keep moving forward. And we have to allow what's behind those walls to move forward, too, even if it's without us.

Maybe when the walls come down, we'll love what we see. But just as likely, it won't be the same as it was. That is a fact we can either accept, adjust to, or not, depending on what was changed. Or perhaps how m uch *we* changed in the season of its closure.

Maybe we found new attractions to love in the wait, new places to explore. Maybe while we were throwing up our hands and laughing on another ride, our relationship to and perspective of the place we were so attached to shifted as well.

The hard truth is that walls shut us out, necessary or not, and they change us as much as they change what's inside them.

The question is, when the walls go up, when we are pulled apart from the people we thought were permanent fixtures, how long do we wait on the other side, hoping to catch a glimpse of what will be when we have access to them again?

And if the attraction closes forever, will we have wasted our lives peeking through fences instead of moving on to find all the joy waiting for us in other lands?

The beautiful thing is you get to choose.

You can't control the closures, the changes, or the consequences of others' decisions. But you *can* control how you respond. You get to choose if your feet stand still or walk away or come back. You get to choose what other attraction you ride.

You get to choose.

Just know that whatever you choose, you are worthy of much more than waiting by a wall forever.

You are worthy of fireworks and castles and endless slides down icy peaks that steal your breath.

You are worthy of finding the finished product instead of begging for the broken.

You deserve your happily ever after, even if it wasn't where you thought it would be.

Starting Over

What did Walt Disney do when he'd lost everything?

He started over.

When he was sitting alone in a cold, empty office

eating beans out of a can

because the business he'd created had failed.

When the character he'd believed to be his big break

was ripped away.

When friends and colleagues betrayed him

again and again and again.

He had every justification to give up.

To sit down and say the loss is too great

the pain is too real

the hope is all lost.

We sing catchy songs about Walt having a suitcase and a dream but when everything you own is in a bag in your hand

it looks more like a nightmare.

Yet every step forward you take

while clutching remnants of the life you thought you'd have

is brave

is defining

because you can't coast into a new life

you are *birthed into it.*

The pain of surrender

will be what builds your home.

The ashes of what was

are not swept away

but built upon

as you set down your suitcase on the floor of your new life

because you finally learned to let go.

Author's Note

This book was a unique one, as it was written over the course of a year at the same time as I wrote my fiction book *Who the Mirror Reflects*. Those who have read that book might recognize some similar themes between that one and this: the idea of when to stay with someone you love and when to walk away, hanging onto hope in difficult seasons, learning to trust again after being hurt, and how we perceive our own worthiness.

I wasn't attempting some magical feat of writing two books at once, it just so happened that some days I felt more like writing fiction, and some days I needed to be free to process through something I was thinking about. Subsequently, these two books were birthed together and have some overlap, not unlike the creation process of Pirates of the Caribbean and the Haunted Mansion. While the Imagineers were developing those two iconic attractions, they lost Walt Disney when he passed away (rather suddenly) in 1966, a few months before Pirates was slated to open and almost three before the Haunted Mansion would welcome its first foolish mortal. It left the team reeling, asking "What would Walt do?" and stumbling in the dark as they tried to find their way forward when everything they knew had changed.

Writing these two books has felt exactly like that season for me. Though I didn't lose an icon like Walt, I lost someone who had been an important figure in my life since I was young, and it destabilized my world. I found myself questioning everything, and wandering in a dark forest and not sure how to come out of it.

So I wrote.

And wrote.

And wrote.

And with each word I penned, I started to find myself again. Set my feet in the dirt and proclaimed that I was valuable, even if others treated me like I wasn't. I learned how to set boundaries, and how to be brave enough to risk losing people I loved again, even though it was terrifying.

These words that I wrote are what set me free.

I hope they can do the same for anyone else who has felt less than, hurt, used, abandoned, invisible, and hopeless.

What I've discovered over this past, painful year is that we can create our own light. We are the ones who are capable of illuminating our own world, even when the Shadow Man creeps around and tries to stomp on our fireflies.

We each get to be our own glimmer of pixie dust, and the only thing we need to fly is the belief that we *can*. That the darkness won't last forever. That we will find our way back to a place where we sparkle, bit by bit.

But the most beautiful thing is that we don't have to make that journey alone. When we are struggling to spy that second star to the right because it's gotten cloudy, that's when our friends grab our hand and help us find our way forward. They are the makeshift Fairy Godmothers of our story, ones we are more worthy of than we often believe we are.

I've had so many people who were exactly that for me as I wrote this book.

To my Disney community, Pocketfam, who have gotten me through some tough days just by being the wonderful Disney nerds that you are.

To my Disney content creator colleagues Kirk and Lemuel, who remind me every day to keep running the marathon and keep creating, even when the finish line feels much too far away.

To my greater Disney Cicerone community everywhere that has found me in DMs, emails, comment sections, and even at the parks with encouragement to "keep going." Telling me how my words have impact. Reminding me that what I do matters.

To my early readers who helped me refine my words and make them more impactful: Thank you, from the bottom of my heart. Bri, Katie O., AllyBeth, Jacque, Rhonda, Janis, Mel, and Eliot, your care and attention to these words is so greatly appreciated. You sprinkled your own touch of pixie dust into this book, and it wouldn't be the same without you.

To my three wonderful kids, you are the brightest light in my life. As you grow up and move on to each new season of your lives, I hope these words are something you can carry with you to remind you that you are worthy, loved, and seen, especially in seasons when the world feels dark or heavy.

To my parents, who took me to Disney when I was two so that I would return when I was 20 (and 30, and 40, and...). And to my aunt Diane and mother-in-law Mary Helen who cheer me on from afar even though they aren't "Disney people," know that your support has meant so very much to me.

And last but never least, to Eliot, who's loved me through tattered rags and broken pumpkins. You gave me a stuffed whale to hug when I was stuck, and listened when I talked in circles. Thank you for seeing me, for loving me, for choosing me every day. I am so grateful to get to be your Evangeline, sparkling in the dark next to you.

About the Author

As the owner and creator of Disney Cicerone, Kate is passionate about helping others experience Disney in more meaningful and magical ways, allowing them to fully understand why their love of Disney has personal and social value. Her writing and creative work explore the sociological, psychological, emotional, historical, and unique ways Disney's history and culture influence our lives. When not wandering in the Disney parks looking at rocks and crates, you can find Kate researching, writing, and posting on social media about obscure Disney history with a dash of encouragement.

ALSO BY KATE GRASSO

Books

A Glimpse of the Magic: Finding Ourselves in the Disney Story (Moments of Magic Book 1)
This curated collection of musings about Disney is infused with obscure history that will inspire you to see the parks you love in a new way, encouraging you to slow down, look closer, and see your own story reflected in every magical moment.

Where the Fireflies Dance (Pixie Dust in the Parks Book 1)
Disney history comes alive as two live streamers find love in the shadow of Sleeping Beauty Castle. But with one of them hiding a dangerous secret, their fairy tale romance might just unravel into an unhappily ever after. (@LeahMeTotheMagic & @LucaDisNerd's Story)

What the Mansion Eyes See (Pixie Dust in the Parks Book 2)
Two Disney history live streamers fall in love beneath the watchful eyes of the Haunted Mansion. But as their past begins to haunt their present, what they fear most might just follow them home. (@CreativelyColette & @EricOnTheHunt's story)

Who the Mirror Reflects (Pixie Dust in the Parks Book 3)
Two Disney history-loving cast members find each other in the reflection of the Rivers of America in the Magic Kingdom. But soon their perception of their relationship becomes distorted by their past. As their inner villains threaten to pull them apart, they discover that choosing love even when it's hard is the most magical gift of all. (@SuitcaseAnnaDream & @HenryAroundtheWorld's story)

Be the first to hear about upcoming books

Follow me on Amazon & social media to be the first to hear about what I'm writing next!

Social

For daily obscure Disney History with a dash of encouragement, follow me @disneycicerone on TikTok, Instagram, Facebook, and YouTube!

Podcast

Distory with Kate & Kirk

Exploring the history of the Disney Parks (with a dash of the ridiculous!), the Distory with Kate and Kirk Podcast is an adventure into the fascinatingly obscure details that have made the Disney parks what they are today.

Blog & Website

Want to read more?
Visit the Disney Cicerone blog at disneycicerone.com

Contact

Questions about Disney? I'd love to hear from you!
Contact me anytime at disneycicerone@gmail.com

BIBLIOGRAPHY

Bossert, David. Claude Coats: Walt Disney's Imagineer: The Making of Disneyland: From Toad Hall to the Haunted Mansion and Beyond. First edition. ed. Valencia: The Old Mill Press, Inc., 2021.

Crump, Rolly. It's Kind of a Cute Story. Bamboo Forest Publishing, 2012.

"Daveland," https://davelandweb.com/disneyland/#google_vignette (accessed April 2, 2025).

Deja, Andreas. "Deja View," https://andreasdeja.blogspot.com/2011/07/bill-tytla.html (accessed April 2, 2025).

Docter, Pete and Christopher Merritt. Marc Davis' in His Own Words: Imagineering the Disney Theme Parks. Vol. 1, 2 vols. Los Angeles: Disney Editions, 2019.

Docter, Pete and Christopher Merritt. Marc Davis' in His Own Words: Imagineering the Disney Theme Parks. Vol. 2, 2 vols. Los Angeles: Disney Editions, 2019.

Gennawey, Sam. The Disneyland Story: The Unofficial Guide to the Evolution of Walt Disney's Dream. Keen Communications, 2014.

Ghez, Didier. The Hidden Art of Disney's Mid-Century Era: The 1950s and 1960s. They Drew as They Pleased. San Francisco: Chronicle Books, 2018.

Ghez, Didier et al. Walt's People: Talking Disney with the Artists Who Knew Him. Edited by Didier Ghez. Vol. 1: Xlibris Corporation, 2005.

Ghez, Didier et al. Walt's People: Talking Disney with the Artist Who Knew Him. Edited by Didier Ghez. Vol. 4: Xlibris Corporation, 2007.

Ghez, Didier et al. Walt's People: Talking Disney with the Artists Who Knew Him. Edited by Didier Ghez. Vol. 10: Xlibris Corporation, 2011.

Green, Amy Boothe and Howard E. Green. Remembering Walt: Favorite Memories of Walt Disney. 1st ed. New York: Hyperion, 1999.

Hench, J. (1978). Disneyland is Good for You. C. Haas. New West Magazine: 13-19.

Holt, Nathalia. The Queens of Animation: The Untold Story of the Women Who Transformed the World of Disney and Made Cinematic History. 1st ed. New York: Little, Brown and Company, 2019.

Iwerks, Leslie. The Imagineering Story: The Official Biography of Walt Disney Imagineering. Burbank: Disney Editions, 2022.

Johnson, David. Snow White's People: An Oral History of the Disney Film Snow White and the Seven Dwarfs. Edited by Didier Ghez. Vol. 1: Theme Park Press, 2017.

Johnson, David. Snow White's People: An Oral History of the Disney Film Snow White and the Seven Dwarfs. Edited by Didier Ghez. Vol. 2: Theme Park Press, 2017.

Kothenschulte, Daniel, Walt Disney Archives, Walt Disney Animation Research Library, and Taschen (Firm). The Walt Disney Film Archives: The Animated Movies 1921-1968. Köln: Taschen, 2016.

Mongello, Lou. The Disney Interviews. Vol. 1: Second Star Media, 2020.

Nolte, Foxx. Boundless Realms: Deep Explorations inside Disney's Haunted Mansion. Inklingwood Press, 2020.

Nunis, Richard. Walt's Apprentice: Keeping the Disney Dream Alive. Burbank: Disney Editions, 2022.

Olson, Dan. "Long Forgotten." Last modified December 11, 2023, Accessed January 12, 2024. https://longforgottenhauntedmansion.blogs pot.com/.

Peri, Don, Pete Docter, and George Lucas. Directing at Disney: The Original Directors of Walt's Animated Films. First hardcover edition. ed. Los Angeles: Disney Editions, 2024.

Rafferty, Kevin P. Magic Journey: An Imagineering Fairy Tale. 1st ed. Glendale, CA: Disney Editions, 2019.

Sklar, Marty. Travels with Figment: On the Road in Search of Disney Dreams. First hardcover edition. ed. Glendale, California: Disney Editions, 2019.

Snow, Richard. Disney's Land. New York: Scribner, 2019.

Surrell, Jason. The Disney Mountains: Imagineering at Its Peak. 1st ed. New York, NY: Disney Editions, 2007.

Surrell, Jason. Pirates of the Caribbean: From the Magic Kingdom to the Movies. 1st ed. New York: Disney Editions, 2005.

Thomas, Bob. Walt Disney: An American Original. New York, NY: Hyperion, 1994.

Bossert, David. Claude Coats: Walt Disney's Imagineer: The Making of Disneyland: From Toad Hall to the Haunted Mansion and Beyond. First edition. ed. Valencia: The Old Mill Press, Inc., 2021.

Crump, Rolly. It's Kind of a Cute Story. Bamboo Forest Publishing, 2012.

"Daveland," https://davelandweb.com/disneyland/#google_vignette (accessed April 2, 2025).

Deja, Andreas. "Deja View," https://andreasdeja.blogspot.com/2011/07/bill-tytla.html (accessed April 2, 2025).

Docter, Pete and Christopher Merritt. Marc Davis' in His Own Words: Imagineering the Disney Theme Parks. Vol. 1, 2 vols. Los Angeles: Disney Editions, 2019.

Docter, Pete and Christopher Merritt. Marc Davis' in His Own Words: Imagineering the Disney Theme Parks. Vol. 2, 2 vols. Los Angeles: Disney Editions, 2019.

Gennawey, Sam. The Disneyland Story: The Unofficial Guide to the Evolution of Walt Disney's Dream. Keen Communications, 2014.

Ghez, Didier. The Hidden Art of Disney's Mid-Century Era: The 1950s and 1960s. They Drew as They Pleased. San Francisco: Chronicle Books, 2018.

Ghez, Didier et al. Walt's People: Talking Disney with the Artists Who Knew Him. Edited by Didier Ghez. Vol. 1: Xlibris Corporation, 2005.

Ghez, Didier et al. Walt's People: Talking Disney with the Artist Who Knew Him. Edited by Didier Ghez. Vol. 4: Xlibris Corporation, 2007.

Ghez, Didier et al. Walt's People: Talking Disney with the Artists Who Knew Him. Edited by Didier Ghez. Vol. 10: Xlibris Corporation, 2011.

Green, Amy Boothe and Howard E. Green. Remembering Walt: Favorite Memories of Walt Disney. 1st ed. New York: Hyperion, 1999.

Hench, J. (1978). Disneyland is Good for You. C. Haas. New West Magazine: 13-19.

Holt, Nathalia. The Queens of Animation: The Untold Story of the Women Who Transformed the World of Disney and Made Cinematic History. 1st ed. New York: Little, Brown and Company, 2019.

Iwerks, Leslie. The Imagineering Story: The Official Biography of Walt Disney Imagineering. Burbank: Disney Editions, 2022.

Johnson, David. Snow White's People: An Oral History of the Disney Film Snow White and the Seven Dwarfs. Edited by Didier Ghez. Vol. 1: Theme Park Press, 2017.

Johnson, David. Snow White's People: An Oral History of the Disney Film Snow White and the Seven Dwarfs. Edited by Didier Ghez. Vol. 2: Theme Park Press, 2017.

Kothenschulte, Daniel, Walt Disney Archives, Walt Disney Animation Research Library, and Taschen (Firm). The Walt Disney Film Archives: The Animated Movies 1921-1968. Köln: Taschen, 2016.

Mongello, Lou. The Disney Interviews. Vol. 1: Second Star Media, 2020.

Nolte, Foxx. Boundless Realms: Deep Explorations inside Disney's Haunted Mansion. Inklingwood Press, 2020.

Nunis, Richard. Walt's Apprentice: Keeping the Disney Dream Alive. Burbank: Disney Editions, 2022.

Olson, Dan. "Long Forgotten." Last modified December 11, 2023, Accessed January 12, 2024. https://longforgottenhauntedmansion.blogs pot.com/.

Peri, Don, Pete Docter, and George Lucas. Directing at Disney: The Original Directors of Walt's Animated Films. First hardcover edition. ed. Los Angeles: Disney Editions, 2024.

Rafferty, Kevin P. Magic Journey: An Imagineering Fairy Tale. 1st ed. Glendale, CA: Disney Editions, 2019.

Sklar, Marty. Travels with Figment: On the Road in Search of Disney Dreams. First hardcover edition. ed. Glendale, California: Disney Editions, 2019.

Snow, Richard. Disney's Land. New York: Scribner, 2019.

Surrell, Jason. The Disney Mountains: Imagineering at Its Peak. 1st ed. New York, NY: Disney Editions, 2007.

Surrell, Jason. Pirates of the Caribbean: From the Magic Kingdom to the Movies. 1st ed. New York: Disney Editions, 2005.

Thomas, Bob. Walt Disney: An American Original. New York, NY: Hyperion, 1994.

Made in the USA
Columbia, SC
09 June 2025

59118683R00174